Practical Problems in Research Methods

A Casebook with Questions for Discussion

Estabrook D. Verdugo

 Pyrczak Publishing
P.O. Box 39731 • Los Angeles, CA 90039

Although the author and publisher have made every effort to ensure the accuracy and completeness of information contained in this book, we assume no responsibility for errors, inaccuracies, omissions, or any inconsistency herein. Any slights of people, places, or organizations are unintentional.

Cover design by Michael Henderson.

Editorial assistance provided by Elaine Fuess, Sharon Young, Brenda Koplin, and Randall R. Bruce.

Printed in the United States of America.
10 9 8 7 6 5 4 3 2   DOC   04 03 02 01 00 99 98

ISBN 1-884585-11-6

Table of Contents

Continued →

Notes:

Introduction

This book presents 53 problematic cases from published research in the social and behavioral sciences. For each case, you are presented with a practical problem faced by a researcher and the solution he or she selected. The questions following the cases encourage you to evaluate the solutions that were selected and to consider alternatives.

By using this book, you will learn that research is a dynamic process—that for many practical problems in research methods, there are competing solutions, each with its own advantages and drawbacks.

The Audience for This Book

The cases in this book were drawn from the fields of sociology, psychology, education, and public health with an eye toward research issues typically covered in a first-semester course in research methods.

It is assumed that you are using a standard research methods textbook in which broad principles for conducting research are covered. This book is designed as a supplement to such textbooks in that it provides many more detailed cases than are found in them. The cases illustrate research problems usually described in research methods textbooks such as respondents' tendency to give socially desirable answers, potential respondents' failure to participate in surveys, protecting research participants from possible harm, forming appropriate comparison groups for use in an experiment, and so on.

A Note on Statistics

This book emphasizes the design, execution, and interpretation of empirical studies. It does *not* cover issues regarding the analysis of data. Hence, you will find very few statistics in this book. For those of you who need practice in reading and interpreting statistical reporting, I recommend Zealure C. Holcomb's *Interpreting Basic Statistics: A Guide and Workbook Based on Excerpts from Journal Articles* (Pyrczak Publishing).

The Field Tests

This book was thoroughly field-tested at a large state university with students majoring in the social and behavioral sciences. They considered most of the short cases in small groups of three or four, attempting to reach a consensus on the answers. This was followed by a class discussion of the various groups' answers. Most of the longer cases were assigned for homework, followed by a class discussion of answers at the next class meeting. Because the cases are problematic, the students often disagreed initially with each other on the best solutions to the research problems; almost as often, they finally came to a consensus on what they would do if they were conducting the research. Students reported enjoying this interactive process and indicated that the activities stimulated by the material in this book made their research methods classes more meaningful. I hope your reactions to this book are equally positive.

Acknowledgment

I am grateful to Patricia Bates Simun of California State University, Los Angeles for her many helpful comments on the first draft of this book.

Estabrook D. Verdugo

Section I

Short Cases

Part A

Sampling

Case 1

Sampling Hispanic Adults by Telephone[1]

Problem: Researchers wanted to determine how aware adult Hispanics in the San Francisco area are of product warning messages and signs concerning cigarettes, alcoholic beverages, and other consumer products. The researchers needed to contact a sample of them to interview.

A Solution: "Respondents were sampled using…random digit dialing. This procedure…avoids the use of directories with their inherent problem of the exclusion of unlisted numbers while guaranteeing equal probability of selection for all telephone numbers. Such an approach has been used in a number of telephone surveys with Hispanics and has been shown to be not only feasible but also very efficient…

"A household was considered to be eligible if those answering the telephone self-identified as Hispanics. Within a given household, the respondent was selected by asking for the Hispanic resident who had most recently celebrated a birthday and who was between 18 and 65 years of age. Interviews were conducted in the language of preference of the respondent (English or Spanish) by bilingual, bicultural interviewers."

Your Opinions:

1. Note that using random digit dialing gives all telephone numbers, including unlisted numbers, an equal chance of being dialed. Does this procedure give all adult Hispanics in the San Francisco area an equal chance of being selected for the study? Explain.

2. Are there any problems with using self-identification as a Hispanic as a criterion for eligibility to participate in the study? Explain.

3. Speculate on why the interviewer asked to speak with the Hispanic resident between 18 and 65 years of age who had *most recently celebrated a birthday*.

4. Would you be interested in knowing whether some Hispanics who answered the phone refused to be interviewed? Explain.

---

[1] Source/reference: Marín, G. (1994). Self-reported awareness of the presence of product warning messages and signs by Hispanics in San Francisco. *Public Health Reports, 109,* 275–283.

Case 2

Using a Sample of Convenience[1]

Problem: Professors often use samples of college students as participants in their research because they are convenient. Using such samples can be problematic.

An Example: A researcher was interested in women's preferences for married names (*traditional*—taking the husbands' surnames and *nontraditional*—retaining their surnames or hyphenating the two surnames). The researchers surveyed 150 unmarried women students enrolled in an introductory psychology course. They asked the women to indicate what they would do, assuming that their husbands had no opinion on the matter. They were told "If you have not thought much about this issue, please consider it now and give your opinion even if you are not 100% certain." They were also asked to give the reasons for their name choice. Almost 60% of the women chose to take the husband's name. In their conclusion, the researchers noted that "one of the most striking results of this study is many respondents' unquestioning attitudes toward" taking the husband's surname as indicated by the fact that many gave responses such as "I don't know, I guess it's tradition," or simply writing the word "tradition" as their reason.

Your Opinions:

1. Because of the nature of the sample, this study provides information on what women *plan to do*. Do you think this is as interesting as gathering information on what a sample of married women have done? Explain.

2. The researchers apparently suspected that some participants in this sample may not have given the issue much thought before participating in the study and might not be certain of their opinion. In light of this, would it have been interesting to have the students rate the degree of certainty they had in their answers? Explain.

3. What is your opinion on having the women assume their husbands had no opinion? (Note that because of the nature of the sample, the researchers either needed to provide an assumption on this matter or allow the participants to make their own assumptions.)

4. Are you surprised by the "unquestioning attitudes toward name traditions"?

---

[1] Source/reference: Twenge, J. M. (1997). "Mrs. his name": Women's preferences for married names. *Psychology of Women Quarterly, 21*, 417–429.

Case 3

Using Quota Sampling[1]

Problem: Professors with limited resources usually find it difficult to obtain adequate samples of the general adult population for their research. Instead, many study samples of college students, who are readily available, even though there is no reason to believe that samples of college students are representative of the national population of adults. (Of course, often professors are interested in the behavior of college students only, in which case, using college students is not a problem.)

A Solution: "In order to reach a wide range of people, the data were collected using a purposive, quota design. Students enrolled in a research methods class…were given course credit for collecting the data for this study. These research assistants were…instructed to recruit adults (not college students) that they knew in six age and gender quotas (male and female: 18–34, 35–49, and 50 and older) to complete questionnaires. Because the students were given their assignment in the weeks prior to spring break, most of them contacted adults from their home areas. The adult respondents completed the written self-administered questionnaires. The research assistants returned a total of 566 questionnaires."

Your Opinions:

1. Speculate on why the research assistants were told to recruit adults who were "not college students."

2. Do you think that the researcher achieved her goal of reaching a "wide range of people"? Explain.

3. Do you think that the sample is probably representative of the adult population of the United States? Explain.

4. In addition to gender and age, are there other variables for which quotas could have been established that would improve the sample?

---

[1] Source/reference: Perse, E. M. (1996). Sensation seeking and the use of television for arousal. *Communication Reports*, *9*, 37–48.

Case 4

Using an Incentive to Increase Response Rate[1]

Problem: When attempting to interview members of the general population, a substantial percentage of the sample often refuses to be interviewed.

A Solution: Researchers sent a letter to a random sample of households indicating that an interviewer would be calling on them. As an incentive, the researchers included a gift-boxed ball point pen (imprinted with the words "University of Michigan" in gold) along with a note saying that the pen was a token of appreciation for participating in the upcoming interview.

Drawbacks to the Solution: The cost of the study was increased by $3.98 ($3.75 for the pen and $0.23 for additional postage) per potential respondent contacted. In addition, the incentive might "alter the composition of the responding sample." For example, it might be more effective gaining the participation of people from low socioeconomic status groups than higher socioeconomic groups. Furthermore, an incentive might alter the way in which respondents answered the questions, which asked about demographic variables, participants' recollection of recent events in history, and their attitudes toward social issues.

Your Opinions:

1. Do you think it would be better to send a letter offering a pen only to those who complete the interviews instead of giving away the pens to all potential respondents before the interviewers contact them? Explain.

2. In your opinion, how serious is the possible drawback that the incentive might "alter the composition of the responding sample"? Explain.

3. If you had received the gift pen, would you be likely to alter your answers to the questions because of it? For example, would you be more likely to try to "please the interviewer" by giving answers you think might please him or her? Explain.

4. Are there other relatively inexpensive gifts that might be used as incentives? If yes, name some. Are they likely to be as effective as a gift pen? Explain.

---

[1] Source/reference: Willimack, D. K., Schuman, H., Pennell, B., & Lepkowski, J. M. (1995). Effects of a prepaid nonmonetary incentive on response rates and response quality in a face-to-face survey. *Public Opinion Quarterly, 59,* 78–92.

Case 5

Obtaining a Sample of Psychotherapy Clients[1]

Problem: Researchers wanted to survey "a large, diverse sample of psychotherapy patients" for a study of the patients' positive and negative evaluations of being physically touched by psychotherapists.

A Solution: The researchers decided to draw a sample of therapists and have them distribute anonymous questionnaires to their patients (neither the patients' nor therapists' names were to be placed on the questionnaires). "A list of therapists in a large Southern metropolitan area was generated from state professional association and telephone directories of therapists…(and upon recommendation of therapists and respondents, expanded to include therapists in other states). Over 300 therapists were contacted. Of the 900 [questionnaires] distributed, approximately 125 were mailed to cities and mid-sized towns in other states in the Midwest, the Northeast, and the Southeast." Two hundred thirty-one usable questionnaires were returned.

Your Opinions:

1. In your opinion, was the researchers' method of sampling likely to result in "a large, diverse sample" of patients? Explain.

2. Two hundred thirty-one of the 900 questionnaires were returned. Does this cause a sampling problem? Could it affect the results? Explain.

3. The researchers state that over 300 therapists were contacted, but they do not indicate how many agreed to distribute questionnaires. As a consumer of research, would you be interested in having this information? Why?

4. The therapists knew the purpose of the study and the contents of the questionnaires. Is it possible that some of the therapists felt threatened by the study even though the patients' responses were to be anonymous? Is this a serious threat to the study? Explain.

---

[1] Source/reference: Horton, J. A., Clance, P. R., Sterk-Elifson, C., Emshoff, J. (1995). Touch in psychotherapy: A survey of patients' experiences. *Psychotherapy, 32*, 443–457.

Section I

Short Cases

Part B

Measurement

Case 6

Measuring the Attractiveness of Participants[1]

Problem: Researchers wanted to study the relationship between facial attractiveness and social variables in a sample of 60 male and 65 female undergraduates. A valid measure of facial attractiveness was needed.

The Measure: "Participants posed for a photograph, for which they would receive $3.00. ...facial photographs were taken of each participant from a distance of 3 feet... Participants were not warned in advance about being photographed so that they would not go out of their way to dress up or primp, thereby yielding a different look from their usual appearance. Physical attractiveness was rated by 57 students (27 men and 30 women) at a different university in the same part of the country. Because there were too many slides to be judged in a single session, the slides were randomly split into two sets. Each slide was rated by approximately half of the judges in sessions lasting approximately 50 minutes. To familiarize raters with the range of photographs, judges were first shown the entire set of slides to be rated. Actual ratings followed, with raters having 25 seconds to rate each slide. No communication was permitted during the session. Slides were grouped by sex, with half the judges seeing the male slides first and the other half seeing the female slides first. Two different random orders were used within each set. Judges were instructed to use their own standards of attractiveness and to rate slides of each target participant on a 1 (very unattractive) to 15 (very attractive) scale. In the analyses reported later in this article, the average rating of each slide was used. These averages were normally distributed and ranged from 2.09 to 12.16, with a mean of 6.96 ($SD = 2.05$)."

Your Opinions:

1. The attractiveness of each participant was rated by about half the 57 judges, and their average rating was used in the analysis. Does it seem worthwhile to use such a large number of judges? Explain.

2. Speculate on why students at a different university were used as judges and why half the judges were shown the male slides first.

3. What is your overall opinion on the measurement procedure? Is there anything you would change? Explain.

---

[1] Source/reference: Tidwell, M. O., Reis, H. T., & Shaver, P. R. (1996). Attachment, attractiveness, and social interaction: A diary study. *Journal of Personality and Social Psychology, 71*, 729–745. Copyright © 1996 by the American Psychological Association, Inc.

Case 7

Measuring Social Desirability[1]

Problem: Researchers wanted to study the masculine socialization process, including fear of intimacy, using a variety of self-report measures administered to 208 undergraduate men. The researchers were concerned that some respondents might give *socially desirable responses* (responses the men believed would be approved of by society) rather than responses that reflect their true feelings.

A Solution: In addition to the other self-report measures, the researchers administered a measure of social desirability. "The tendency to respond in a socially desirable way was assessed with a 13-item short version…of the 33-item Marlow-Crowne Social Desirability Scale… Participants read statements describing socially desirable (or undesirable, for reverse-scored items) behaviors (e.g., 'No matter who I'm talking to, I'm always a good listener.') and mark them either true or false, with higher scores indicating more socially desirable responding."

Your Opinions:

1. Do you agree that someone who answers "true" to the item shown above might be responding in a socially desirable way?

2. Suppose a participant answered most of the 13 items in a socially desirable direction. Would you be willing to take this as evidence that he or she may also be responding in a socially desirable direction on other measures such as a scale with questions on men's fear of intimacy? Explain.

3. If you were conducting the research, would you omit a participant who scored very high on the social desirability scale from the analyses of the other variables? Explain.

4. Speculate on what the authors mean by "or undesirable, for reverse-scored items." Write an item that describes a socially undesirable behavior that might be included in a social desirability scale.

---

[1] Source/reference: Fischer, A. R., & Good, G. E. (1997). Men and psychotherapy: An investigation of alexithymia, intimacy, and masculine gender roles. *Psychotherapy*, *34*, 160–170.

Case 8

Measuring Students' Distant Memories[1]

Problem: Researchers wanted to learn more about "sexual liaisons between students and educators during doctoral training in clinical or counseling psychology."

A Solution: Selected members of the American Psychological Association were mailed a questionnaire. The items on the questionnaire were drawn from questionnaires used in previous studies. However, "although the original wording of these questions was retained wherever possible, some items were altered to reduce biased language. For example, [earlier researchers] had asked about the degree of coercion respondents felt existed in the relationship. Levels of coercion were used as anchors at each end of the scale (ranging from *very coerced* to *not at all coerced*). The choices in the present study ranged from 1 (*very coerced*) to 5 (*entirely voluntary*). Additionally, a midpoint was added to each scale, representing ambivalence or a mixed positive and negative response.

"On average, respondents received their doctorates 14 years ago. This time lapse raises the possibility that participants forgot or that they gave distorted or otherwise inaccurate responses because of the passage of time. Thus, readers should be cautious in interpreting these data."

Your Opinions:

1. Do you agree that the choice "entirely voluntary" is less biased than "not at all coerced"? Explain.

2. For the question described above, do you think that including a midpoint choice was a good idea? Explain.

3. In your opinion, how important is the caution regarding the fact that the events that respondents were reporting on happened over 14 years ago?

4. Do you think that some types of events might be remembered more accurately over a long time period than other types of events? Explain.

---

[1] Source/reference: Hammel, G. A., Olkin, R., & Taube, D. O. (1996). Student-Educator Sex in Clinical and Counseling Psychology Doctoral Training. *Professional Psychology: Research and Practice, 27*, 93–97. Copyright © 1996 by the American Psychological Association, Inc.

Case 9

Evaluating an Acculturation Scale[1]

Problem: Researchers wanted to measure the acculturation of samples of Chinese and European Americans. The researchers located a previously published acculturation scale: the Suinn-Lew Asian Self-Identity Acculturation Scale (SL-ASIA). Because they modified the scale for the purposes of their study, what was previously known about its reliability and validity did not strictly apply.

A Solution: The researchers administered the scale to their sample of college students who were Chinese Americans. "Participants used a 5-point Likert-type scale ranging from 1 = *very Asian* to 5 = *very American* to rate 25 multiple-choice items pertaining to their cultural identification, food and entertainment preferences, and language proficiency." As a measure of reliability, they computed Cronbach's alpha and obtained a coefficient of .88. [This coefficient indicates the extent to which the individual items correlate with each other on a scale from 0.00 (no correlation) to 1.00 (perfect correlation)]. In addition, they "examined the relationship between Chinese Americans'…acculturation scores and length of time spent in the United States to assess the concurrent validity of the SL-ASIA. …[They] found that the longer Chinese Americans had lived in the United States, the more acculturated they reported being to mainstream American culture ($r = .75$)…"

The European American sample took the same scale except that *very European* was substituted for *very Asian* in the choices. For this sample, Cronbach's alpha equaled .68, and $r = .47$ for the relationship between the scores and the length of time spent in the United States.

Your Opinions:

1. In your opinion, is the scale reasonably reliable? Explain.

2. Are you convinced that the scale is valid? Explain.

3. Scores on individual items were averaged for each participant so that the total scores on the entire scale for each participant could range from 0 to 5. The Chinese American sample had an average total score of 2.78. For the European Americans, the average was 4.06. Does this information increase your confidence in the validity of the scale? Explain.

---

[1] Source/reference: Tsai, J. L., Levenson, R. W. (1997). Cultural influences on emotional responding: Chinese American and European American dating couples during interpersonal conflict. *Journal of Cross-Cultural Psychology, 28,* 600–625.

Case 10

Determining the Validity of Self-Reports[1]

Problem: Researchers developed a driving while intoxicated (DWI) instructional program that was included in the instruction at a random half of 84 driving schools; the other half served as a control group. While they found that those who received the DWI program had greater knowledge of DWI and favorable attitude change, they found no difference in self-reported driving under the influence.

The validity of the latter finding depends on the validity of the self-reports given on a questionnaire. To check their validity, the researchers took three steps. First, they interviewed friends and family members of the students and asked whether the students had driven while intoxicated. Second, they conducted in-depth telephone interviews with 22 respondents whom the researchers thought were most likely to have driven while intoxicated: those who had admitted on the pretest that they had consumed more than 10 glasses of alcohol on at least one occasion but who stated on the posttest questionnaire that they had not driven while intoxicated after the program. Third, they checked court records of 229 students who had drivers' licenses for a history of DWI offenses that might have occurred after the program.

Your Opinions:

1. What is your opinion of the first step the researchers took? Do you think that it might help identify students who reported they did not drive while intoxicated but actually did? Explain.

2. Do you agree that those who admitted to consuming a large quantity of alcohol on at least one occasion were good targets for the in-depth interviews? Do you think that they were the most likely to drive while intoxicated and fail to admit it? Explain.

3. How useful is it to examine court records given that law enforcement officials catch only some people who drive while intoxicated? Explain.

---

[1] Source/reference: Kayser, R. E., Schippers, G. M., & Van Der Staak, C. P. F. (1995). Evaluation of a Dutch educational "driving while intoxicated (DWI)" prevention program for driving schools. *Journal of Drug Education, 25,* 379–393.

Section I

Short Cases

Part C

Operational Definitions

Case 11

Defining "Physical Abuse" of Children[1]

Problem: In recent years, there has been a dramatic increase in the estimates of physical abuse of children by their parents. For example, there were 669,000 cases reported to social service agencies in 1976; the comparable figure for 1995 is 3,111,000.

"Of considerable importance, the Gallup poll and other population surveys… include ratings of very specific acts that…illustrate how the definition of violence affects estimates of prevalence rates… For instance, if spanking is considered to be violent…, then an estimated two-thirds of children in the United States are victims of abuse. When violence is defined as hitting with an object,…the rate drops to 5%. Naturally, rates become even lower when physical child abuse is defined by increasingly severe actions [such as throwing or knocking a child down, hitting with a fist, and beating up or choking a child].

"…we do want to point out that it is likely that there has been some real increase in child abuse in recent years. Although the number of moderate cases of child abuse remained stable between 1986 and 1993, the number of serious cases…quadrupled… If the increase was solely due to increased awareness or 'definitional creep,'…one would expect increases across all levels of severity."

Your Opinions:

1. Explain in your own words what you think the authors mean by *definitional creep* as it related to child abuse.

2. Is there an advantage to referring to specific acts, as was done in the Gallup poll, when defining child abuse? Explain.

3. If you were conducting research on child abuse, would you include spanking on the bottom as a form of abuse in your definition? Explain.

4. In addition to the possibility of a changing definition over time, could the increase in reported cases also be attributed, in part, to the public's awareness of the issue? Explain.

---

[1] Source/reference: Emery, R. E., & Laumann-Billings, L. (1998). An overview of the nature, causes, and consequences of abusive family relationships. *American Psychologist, 53,* 121–135. Copyright © 1998 by the American Psychological Association, Inc.

Case 12

Defining "Economic Well-Being"[1]

Problem: Economic well-being is a variable that is widely studied in the social and behavioral sciences. How it is defined can have an important effect on the results of the studies.

Two Definitions: "Recent studies of poverty most commonly define poverty by cash income, using the federal poverty threshold as a marker. Because the index is an absolute dollar amount, not a percentage of the median income nor a percentile, it is theoretically possible for everyone to be above the poverty threshold.

"Unlike poverty status, SES [socioeconomic status] signifies an individual's, a family's, or a group's ranking on a hierarchy according to its access to or control over some combination of valued commodities such as wealth, power, and social status... Dispute exists among social scientists about how SES should be defined and measured, but there is agreement that parental occupation, parental education, family income, prestige, power, and a certain lifestyle are important components of SES... In addition to being multidimensional rather than unidimensional and to denoting relative position rather than status defined by an absolute standard, SES is considerably less volatile than poverty status. During adulthood, SES indicators such as educational attainment and occupational status are less likely to change markedly from one year to the next than is income...

"These distinctions between SES and income poverty are conceptually important and are viewed as crucial for public-policy discussions... Some research has indicated, for example, that poverty and income status have effects on children's development independent of parental education."

Your Opinions:

1. In your opinion, what are some of the advantages and disadvantages of defining economic well-being as poverty indicated by cash income when conducting research?

2. What are some of the advantages and disadvantages of defining economic well-being in terms of SES? Explain.

3. In general, do you think that studies of the effects of well-being defined as poverty or defined as SES are more interesting and informative? Explain.

---

[1] Source/reference: McLoyd, V. C. (1998). Socioeconomic disadvantage and child development. *American Psychologist, 53,* 185–204. Copyright © 1998 by the American Psychological Association, Inc.

Case 13

Defining "Substance Abuse" Among Pregnant Women[1]

Problem: Researchers wanted to identify pregnant women who were substance abusers and compare them with pregnant women who were not substance abusers on a variety of psychological and social variables. Pregnant women who attended an outpatient obstetrics clinic in an inner-city neighborhood were interviewed. The researchers faced this problem: "Because the women in this study were not applying for [drug abuse] treatment and, therefore, [were] not admitted substance abusers and because of the stigma attached to substance abuse during pregnancy, it is probable that some women who were substance abusers were incorrectly classified as nonusers."

A Solution: "A broad definition of substance abuse was used to capture women who had a history of abuse but were reluctant to admit to use in the past 30 days. For instance, women who were bothered by cravings, withdrawal symptoms, or the disturbing effects of alcohol intoxication or drugs were classified as substance abusers even if they denied current use." In addition, women who had ever been treated for drug or alcohol addiction were classified as substance abusers.

Your Opinions:

1. In your opinion, could the procedure described in the solution still fail to identify some of the women who were using substances while they were pregnant? Explain.

2. In your opinion, could the procedure described in the solution lead to the misclassification as a substance abuser who was not a current user? Explain.

3. What is your overall opinion of the solution? If you were conducting the study, would you use it? Explain.

4. Are there other possible solutions that might help solve the problem? Explain.

---

[1] Source/reference: Marcenko, M. O., & Spence, M. Social and psychological correlates of substance abuse among pregnant women. *Social Work Research, 19*, 103–109.

Case 14

Defining a "Social Interaction"[1]

Problem: Researchers wanted to study daily social experience by having participants keep diaries of their social interactions. Because the participants might have varying ideas of what constitutes a social interaction, they were given the definition shown below. *Before reading this definition, consider how you might define a "social interaction."*

The Definition: "An interaction occurs when you and at least one other person pay attention to one another and adjust your behavior to one another. This study is concerned only with interactions that last at least 10 minutes or longer in duration. A conversation is the clearest example of an interaction. Person A says something. Person B responds, and so forth. Dancing and playing games are also interactions. Sitting side by side and watching television is not an interaction unless you are having a running dialogue while the television is on. Listening to a lecture is not an interaction, even if you occasionally ask a question. However, a class discussion group would be an interaction. Let's take a more difficult example. Suppose you are dining with a group of people. You are listening to their conversation but seldom say anything yourself. Do you record this as an interaction? It *is* a social interaction if you are following the conversation *and* could enter into it if you wished. If you are not following the conversation, *or* if it would be inappropriate for you to enter it, it would *not* be recorded as a social interaction. Let's take another difficult example. If you interacted with Person A for an hour, but you are joined by Person B for 20 minutes during the middle third of the hour, *three* interactions should be recorded: A 20-minute interaction with Person A, a 20-minute interaction with both A and B, and a 20-minute interaction with A."

Your Opinions:

1. Compare how you would have defined a social interaction with the researchers' definition. Which definition is better? Explain.

2. In your opinion, is the researchers' definition unambiguous? Explain.

3. Most of the definition consists of examples. Are there enough examples? Can you think of another example that might improve the definition? Explain.

---

[1] Source/reference: Berry, D. S., & Landry, J. C. (1997). Facial maturity and daily social interaction. *Journal of Personality and Social Psychology, 72*, 570–580. Copyright © 1997 by the American Psychological Association, Inc.

Case 15

Defining "Sex" in a National Survey[1]

Problem: Researchers at the National Opinion Research Center at the University of Chicago conducted a major, national survey on sexual behavior, known as the National Health and Social Life Survey, which resulted in various reports as well as a popular book titled *Sex in America: A Definitive Study*. A fundamental problem in this type of research is whether to define "sex" for respondents and, if so, how to define it. The researchers first queried respondents about sex partners with no definition provided for them. For the section asking them to enumerate their sexual partners, the following definition was presented to respondents.

The Definition: "By 'sex' or 'sexual activity,' we mean any mutually voluntary activity with another person that involves genital contact and sexual excitement or arousal, that is, feeling really turned on, even if intercourse or orgasm did not occur.

Please include all persons and times…where you had direct physical contact with the genitals (the sex organs) of someone else and sexual excitement to arousal occurred. Certain activities such as close dancing or kissing without genital contact should NOT be included."

Your Opinions:

1. The researchers enhanced their definition with examples of what is not covered by the definition. In your opinion, how helpful are the examples in framing the definition? Should there be more examples? Explain.

2. Overall, do you think that the definition is operational (i.e., defined in terms of unambiguous physical operations or behaviors)? Explain.

3. In a study of this type, do you think that it is better to provide a definition or to question respondents without giving them a definition? Explain.

4. Suppose that the survey was conducted to estimate how many people are engaging in behaviors that put them at risk for HIV/AIDS. Would the definition shown above be good for such a survey? Explain.

---

[1] Source/reference: Miller, P. V. (1995). They said it couldn't be done: The National Health and Social Life Survey. *Public Opinion Quarterly*, *59*, 404–419.

Section I

Short Cases

Part D

Procedures

Case 16

Controlling the Distribution of a Questionnaire in a Nutrition Study[1]

Problem: Researchers wanted to compare restaurant customers' satisfaction with lower-fat menu items that were promoted during a month-long intervention in restaurants with their satisfaction with regular menu items. Since the resources of the researchers were limited, they were not able to personally distribute the questionnaires to the customers in the eight participating restaurants.

A Solution: The waiters and waitresses were asked to give a questionnaire to customers along with the bill. The researchers visited the restaurants daily to collect the questionnaires and to consult with the management, waiters, and waitresses.

A Drawback to the Solution: "…waitstaff did not distribute the questionnaires as requested. Of the 2,400 questionnaires distributed to restaurants, approximately 900 were given to customers; the 694 returned represented an estimated 10% of customers dining in the restaurants throughout the week. There may have been a systematic bias as respondents from one restaurant represented 30% of total respondents; thus, results may be skewed in favor of that restaurant's clientele. A second source of bias, revealed in follow-up conversations with waitstaff, was that patrons were more likely to receive a questionnaire during quieter times."

Your Opinions:

1. If you had planned this study, would you have anticipated that the waiters and waitresses would distribute the questionnaires to such a small proportion of the customers? Explain.

2. With hindsight, could anything have been done to increase the distribution of the questionnaires by the waiters and waitresses? Are there other ways the questionnaires could have been efficiently and economically distributed? Explain.

3. In your opinion, how serious are the potential biases created by having 30% of the respondents from one of the eight restaurants and by having more of the questionnaires distributed during quieter times?

---

[1] Source/reference: Fitzpatrick, M. P., Chapman, G. E., & Barr, S. I. (1997). Lower-fat menu items in restaurants satisfy customers. *Journal of the American Dietetic Association*, 97, 510–514.

Case 17

Identifying Duplicate Responses to an Anonymous Questionnaire[1]

Problem: Response rates to anonymous questionnaires are often low. Research indicates that a follow-up mailing will sometimes substantially increase the response rate. However, when questionnaires are anonymous, researchers do not know which respondents replied to the first mailing. Thus, a second mailing gives those who replied the first time a chance to respond twice, which may influence the outcome. For example, if those who have strong opinions on the topic of a questionnaire tend to answer the questionnaire twice, then the survey will be biased in favor of those who have strong opinions.

A Solution: Researchers coded each questionnaire returned by health educators with a 1 if it was returned within the first two weeks after the initial mailing or a 2 if it was returned after the first two weeks (when the follow-up questionnaire was mailed). They also wrote on the questionnaire the state from which it was mailed as indicated by the postmark on the return envelope. The questionnaire contained demographic questions on age, sex, race, employment setting, years as a health educator, and years of education. Questionnaires that were coded 1 were compared with those coded 2 for matches on the state from which they were mailed as well as the demographic variables. Those that were matched were considered to be duplicates.

Your Opinions:

1. Are there any potential problems with the solution? Explain.

2. For this technique to work, a researcher must use demographic questions that respondents can answer reliably, that is, give the same answer both times. Do you think that the demographic questions mentioned above can be answered reliably? Are there other ones that might be used to help identify duplicate results?

3. Suppose some respondents mailed the first questionnaire several weeks late and also answered the duplicate questionnaire. Can these respondents be identified? If so, how?

---

[1] Source/reference: Summers, J., & Price, J. H. (1997). Increasing return rates to a mail survey among health educators. *Psychological Reports, 81*, 551–554.

Case 18

Using a Simulated Setting to Evaluate Disciplinary Fairness Training[1]

Problem: Researchers wanted to evaluate a training program for supervisors on how to discipline their unionized employees. The supervisors were taught skills such as using a normal volume and pace in speaking, giving an adequate explanation to the employee, and allowing employees to appeal to a third party to discuss disciplinary procedures. A problem was how to measure these skills realistically in order to compare the trained group with a control group.

A Solution: "When the training of the 35 supervisors was completed, each supervisor in the training and control groups asked a unionized employee to role-play a hypothetical discipline scenario" selected from the following: (a) absenteeism due to a second job, (b) sluggish afternoon performance due to drinking alcohol during lunch hour, (c) sleeping on the job, and (d) tampering with a vending machine. The role-playing was videotaped so that the behaviors could later be evaluated by attorneys who practice labor law as well as by the unionized employees who participated in the role-playing."

Your Opinions:

1. Are there any advantages to using simulated role-playing instead of observing actual disciplinary actions? Explain.

2. Are there any disadvantages to using simulated role-playing instead of observing actual disciplinary actions? Explain.

3. Do you think that a paper-and-pencil questionnaire asking the supervisors how they would handle various disciplinary action scenarios would be more or less valid than the role-playing as a way to gather the needed information?

4. Are there advantages and disadvantages to videotaping the role-playing? Explain.

---

[1] Source/reference: Cole, N. D., & Latham, G. P. (1997). Effects of training in procedural justice on perceptions of disciplinary fairness by unionized employees and disciplinary subject matter experts. *Journal of Applied Psychology, 82,* 699–705.

Case 19

Using Confederates in an Experiment[1]

Problem: Researchers formed two groups of college students that were to make exact duplicates of birthday cards (presented as an industrial task) and receive $1.00 for each card made. Both groups shared supplies that were stored in a supply room. The two groups could communicate with each other via an intercom. One of the groups was actually working for the researchers; in psychological research such individuals are called *confederates*. At the researchers' direction, the confederates hoarded supplies, making it impossible for the students in the other group (who were the real subjects) to complete as many cards as the confederates. As the researchers expected, the subjects followed a standard escalation sequence in their communications over the intercom with the confederates. They first requested that the confederates (whom they presumably thought were just another group of subjects) stop hoarding supplies, then made impatient demands, followed by complaints, angry statements, threats, harassment, and verbal abuse.

Because the subjects knew that they were subjects in a psychological experiment, they might have suspected the true nature of the study (that the other group was actually a group of confederates who were deliberately annoying them), in which case their reactions might not be natural.

Your Opinions:

1. The researchers realized that extreme hoarding by the confederates might not be believable. Thus, they allowed the subjects to have sufficient supplies to complete 3 cards, while the confederates supposedly completed 7 cards. (The production of each group was announced periodically during the study.) Does this seem reasonable? Explain.

2. When the subjects complained to the confederates about their hoarding behavior, the confederates replied with statements prepared by the researchers such as, "I'm still using it," "I'll bring it out when I'm done," and "I still need it because I messed up one of my cards." If you were a subject in this study, would you have found these replies believable? Explain.

3. In your opinion, would it have been worthwhile at the end of the study to ask the subjects whether they suspected that the researchers had set them up? Explain.

---

[1] Source/reference: Mikolic, J. M., Parker, J. C., & Pruitt, D. G. (1997). Escalation in response to persistent annoyance: Groups versus individuals and gender effects. *Journal of Personality and Social Psychology, 72*, 151–163.

Case 20

Working with Severely Angry Participants[1]

Problem: Researchers wished to study the effects of a treatment for anger on severely angry Vietnam War veterans who had posttraumatic stress disorder (PTSD). Major problems were that the participants were potentially dangerous, poor at complying with requests, and prone to drop out of treatment.

Solutions: The researchers' initial design called for role-play provocation tests to enable them "to obtain behavioral ratings of responses to provocation. However, we were unable to recruit assistants to role-play provocation scenes because they were concerned about their personal safety." As alternatives, the researchers asked the participants to keep diaries of their daily anger experiences and asked their spouses or significant others to make daily ratings of participants' anger. Compliance with these requests was so low that the data could not be used.

"We were aware at the outset that high participant dropout is the norm in PTSD treatment research. Vietnam War veterans with PTSD distrust research and often perceive it as exploitative (like military service). We attempted to mitigate this problem systematically. For example, experienced Vietnam War veterans were chosen as therapists in the hope of promoting trust and alliance between participants and therapists. Even this did not always help. One veteran angrily denounced his therapist, who had been frequently in combat as an officer in Vietnam, saying 'anyone knows officers cannot be trusted.'" The dropout rate was 46.4%.

One participant physically assaulted a Vet Center counselor. By the end of the study, he had murdered his girlfriend in a fit of rage. "This is not an isolated example of the potential for violence of the study participants."

Your Opinions:

1. Although the researchers could not apply the measures mentioned above, they did administer other measures. For example, they gave the participants scripts about hypothetical situations that might provoke anger such as being cut off abruptly in traffic, while measuring their blood pressure and heart rate as well as asking participants to rate how angry the situations would have made them. Is this a good substitute for the measures called for in the original design?

2. Are there any other steps that might be taken to reduce the danger and encourage the participants to stay in the experimental treatment? Explain.

---

[1] Source/reference: Chemtob, C. M., Novaco, R. W., Hamada, R. S., & Gross, D. M. (1997). Cognitive-behavioral treatment for severe anger in posttraumatic stress disorder. *Journal of Consulting and Clinical Psychology, 65,* 184–189.

Section I

Short Cases

Part E

Experimental/Causal Comparative Designs

Case 21

Selecting Participants for a Comparison of Asian and White Americans[1]

Problem: A researcher wanted to compare Asian Americans and White Americans on variables such as depression and social anxiety. Identifying two groups that are comparable except for race is essential to avoid confounding. For example, if highly educated Asian Americans are compared with poorly educated White Americans, differences in anxiety between the two groups may be due to either the difference in education *or* the difference in race.

Selection of the Participants: "The sample for this study consisted of 348 university students enrolled in introductory psychology courses at the University of California, Los Angeles. There were 183 self-identified non-Hispanic White American participants (84 men, 99 women). Those White participants who were not born in the United States were excluded from the study to maintain cultural homogeneity in the group.

"Of the 165 self-identified Asian American participants (76 men, 89 women), 100 were Chinese American, 52 were Korean American, and 13 were Japanese American. The Asian American group was predominantly foreign-born, with approximately two-thirds ($n = 110$, 67%) listing their place of birth in Asia. This high percentage of foreign-born Asian Americans in the sample is consistent with the 1990 Census data, which listed 64% of Asians/Pacific Islanders as foreign-born... Of the remaining U.S.-born Asian Americans, most ($n = 49$, 31% of Asian group) were second generation (i.e., one or both parents born in Asia), with a very small number of Asian Americans being third generation ($n = 3$, 2% of Asian group) and fourth generation ($n = 3$, 2% of Asian group). Among the foreign-born Asian Americans, the mean age of entry into the United States was 8.2 years old ($SD = 5.0$), and the mean number of years spent in the United States was 13.8 years ($SD = 4.9$)."

Your Opinions:

1. What is your opinion on excluding White participants who were foreign born?

2. What is your opinion on the comparability of the two groups? Would you like to have additional information on their comparability? Explain.

---

[1] Source/reference: Okazaki, S. (1997). Sources of ethnic differences between Asian American and White American college students on measures of depression and social anxiety. *Journal of Abnormal Psychology*, *106*, 52–60. Copyright © 1997 by the American Psychological Association, Inc.

Forming Experimental and Control Groups in a Study of Drug Prevention[1]

Problem: Researchers wanted to evaluate a family-participation drug prevention program in the Boys & Girls Clubs. Four clubs were purposively selected to receive the program because they had directors who would strongly support the promotion of family involvement and would give the program coordinator the flexibility to work in nontraditional ways to encourage family participation. This created a problem: A true experimental design could not be used because the program clubs were not selected at random.

A Solution: Other Boys & Girls Clubs that were similar on socioeconomic and other demographic variables to the family-participation program clubs were selected as comparison groups.

A Drawback to the Solution: Children in the family-participation program were about a quarter of a year younger, on the average, than those in the comparison groups. While all groups were predominantly African American, there were differences in the second most frequent racial/ethnic groups with differences in the Hispanic and Caucasian mix. There were differences in the gender composition of the groups (e.g., 35% female in the family-participation clubs and 41% female in the control clubs).

Your Opinions:

1. Is the use of purposively selected clubs (rather than randomly selected clubs) a limitation of the study? Explain.

2. If you answered "yes" to question 1, how serious is the limitation? Explain.

3. Overall, do you believe the solution is better than nothing (that is, not having a control or comparison group)?

4. Are there other possible solutions that might help solve the problem? Explain.

---

[1] Source/reference: St. Pierre, T. L., Mark, M. M., Kaltreider, D. L., & Aikin, K. J. (1997). Involving parents of high-risk youth in drug prevention: A three-year longitudinal study in Boys & Girls Clubs. *Journal of Early Adolescence, 17*, 21–50.

Case 23

Forming Comparison Groups in Classroom Research on Reading[1]

Problem: Researchers wanted to form three groups in an experiment on different methods of teaching.

A Solution: "The six classrooms were randomly assigned to three treatment groups: two experimental groups and one control." In one of the experimental groups, students were taught literacy using literature in addition to standard reading textbooks (known as *basal readers*). In the other experimental group, students were taught literacy in the same way as in the first experimental group but were also taught science using literature as well as science textbooks. The control group students "continued their regular basal reading and science textbook instruction.

"During the study, all classrooms spent 7½ hours a week on reading instruction. In the experimental groups, teachers spent 3½ hours a week with the basal reading materials and 4 hours with literature. In the control group, all 7½ hours a week of reading instruction involved basal materials.

"We used intact classrooms when it was preferable to randomly assign teachers and children to the different conditions. We were unable to make random assignments because we were working in a school district where they made their own decisions about this."

Your Opinions:

1. Six classroom teachers were involved in this study with two teachers using each of the three teaching methods. In your opinion, was this a sufficient number of teachers for a study of this type? Explain.

2. The researchers state that it would have been preferable to assign children at random to the different conditions. Instead, they assigned classrooms at random. In your opinion, is this an important limitation of the study? Explain.

3. The researchers controlled the amount of time spent on reading in the three types of classrooms. Is this important? Explain.

---

[1] Source/reference: Morrow, L. M., Pressley, M., Smith, J. K., & Smith, M. (1997). The effect of a literature-based program integrated into literacy and science instruction with children from diverse backgrounds. *Reading Research Quarterly*, *32*, 54–76.

Case 24

Forming Comparison Groups for a Study of Postpartum Disorders[1]

Problem: Researchers wanted to compare "the mental health and marital quality in a...group of spouses of women with postpartum psychiatric disorders and a control group of men whose wives had recently given birth but had no such disorders."

A Solution: At 6 weeks postpartum, telephone interviews were used to identify women with psychiatric problems and the control women for the study. The couples in the two groups were matched on age, years of education, percentage employed outside the home, and occupational status. "At 6 to 9 weeks postpartum, couples underwent a psychiatric interview and completed self-report measures of psychological symptoms, marital satisfaction, and changes in couple and family functioning since the birth."

Your Opinions:

1. Why do you think the researchers matched on variables such as age?

2. In your opinion, are there any other variables on which the two groups should have been matched? Explain.

3. Differences were found between the control husbands and the husbands of women with postpartum psychiatric disorders. For example, the latter were less satisfied with their marriages, more worried about family responsibilities, and more dissatisfied with changes in household routines. Does this indicate that the women's postpartum disorders *caused* these problems in their husbands? Could it be that husbands with problems helped *cause* their wives postpartum depression? Could other variables be responsible for the differences? Explain.

4. Would the study be stronger if the measures described in the solution had also been administered as pretests at the time the couples were contemplating pregnancy? If yes, explain how this would strengthen the study.

---

[1] Source/reference: Zelkowitz, P., & Milet, T. H. (1996). Postpartum psychiatric disorders: Their relationship to psychological adjustment and marital satisfaction in the spouses. *Journal of Abnormal Psychology, 105*, 281–285.

Case 25

Identifying Comparison Groups for a Study of Childhood Abuse[1]

Problem: Researchers wanted to study the long-term effects of childhood physical and sexual abuse. For this purpose, they needed to identify adult participants who had been abused as children as well as an appropriate control group.

A Solution: "In the first phase of this research, a large group of children who were abused, neglected, or both approximately 20 years ago were followed up through an examination of official juvenile and criminal records and compared with a matched control group of children... The rationale for identifying the abused and neglected group was that their cases were serious enough to come to the attention of the authorities. Only court-substantiated cases of child abuse and neglect were included here. Cases were drawn from the records of county juvenile and adult criminal courts in a metropolitan area in the Midwest during the years 1967 through 1971. To avoid potential problems with ambiguity in the direction of causality and to ensure that temporal sequence was clear (i.e., child abuse or neglect leads to subsequent outcomes), abuse and neglect cases were restricted to those in which children were less than 11 years of age at the time of the abuse or neglect incident. Thus, these are cases of early childhood abuse, neglect, or both."

Your Opinions:

1. Do you think that it was a good idea to limit the study to "court-substantiated cases"? Why? Why not?

2. The researchers planned to use a "matched control group of children." If you were conducting the study, on what variables would you try to match nonabused children with those who had been abused? (For example, they might be matched on race or ethnicity.)

3. Do you agree that it was a good idea to limit the study to children who were less than 11 years of age at the time of the abuse or neglect? Explain.

---

[1] Source/reference: Widom, C. S., & Morris, S. (1997). Accuracy of adult recollections of childhood victimization: Part 2. Childhood sexual abuse. *Psychological Assessment*, *9*, 34–46. Copyright © 1997 by the American Psychological Association, Inc.

Section I

Short Cases

Part F

Protecting the Rights of Participants/Ethical Considerations

Case 26

Using Deception in a Study of Social Interactions[1]

Problem: When researchers study social interactions, they often give participants a reason to interact (such as "discuss the following topic") and observe the participants with their full knowledge and consent. Such researchers take the risk that participants may act unnaturally under these conditions.

A Solution: "Interested individuals signed up for an experiment on 'group processes' in exchange for extra credit points… Participants were informed of the name of their potential partner and asked if they were acquainted. If they were, that individual was assigned to a different partner.

"Participants were greeted by the RA [research assistant], taken to a medium-sized room, and seated on a couch. A video camera was present, and the RA explained that part of the study involved the development of a set of videotapes for future studies of social perception. She then went to the camera, ejected the videotape, and indicated that the wrong tape had been left in the machine. The participants were asked to wait together while the RA left the laboratory, supposedly to retrieve the correct videotape. The pair was left alone for 6 minutes. During that time, they were surreptitiously filmed by a second camera located in a darkened, adjoining equipment room that had been activated by remote control when the RA left. Although they had not been specifically directed to talk with one another, all dyads spontaneously engaged in conversation."

Your Opinions:

1. Since the participants were "interested individuals" who signed up for a study on "group processes," was there an ethical problem with surreptitiously filming their interactions with other participants? Explain.

2. If you answered "yes" to question 1, is there any circumstance in which deception in social and behavioral research might be justified? Explain.

3. Are there other ways the data could have been collected without using deception and surreptitious videotaping? If yes, would other methods yield data as valid as those obtained with surreptitious videotaping? Explain.

---

[1] Source/reference: Berry, D. S., & Hansen, J. S. (1996). Positive affect, negative affect, and social interaction. *Journal of Personality and Social Psychology, 71*, 796–809. Copyright © 1996 by the American Psychological Association, Inc.

Case 27

Prescreening Adolescents for Stress[1]

Problem: Researchers wanted to study pet bereavement among adolescents. An initial problem was to obtain a sample of participants who had experienced the death of a pet within the year previous to the study.

A Solution: "Young people were recruited from local 4-H and Boy Scout organizations, 9th- and 10th-grade classes at area high schools and referrals from friends and colleagues (none of the potential participants was known to any of the investigators, however). The senior investigator spoke privately to each about conditions for participation, invited him or her to join the study, and administered a prescreening instrument.

"To avoid recording spuriously high levels of grief following pet loss, it was important to minimize the effects of other stressful life events. For this reason, each potential participant was screened with the modified Adolescent Life Change Event Scale (ALCES). The ALCES is a 24-item, self-report measure of stress that has been validated for individuals ranging in age from 12 to 29 years... Items consist of a rank-order listing of potential life changes that are known to be stressful (pet loss is ranked 11th). Anyone who marked any item more stressful than pet loss was excluded from participation in the study.

"After the prescreening, those who remained in the study were given the instrument package and provided with directions for completing it. They were also provided with consent forms to be signed by a parent or guardian and stamped, addressed envelopes for returning completed questionnaires."

Your Opinions:

1. In your opinion, is there any potential for harm by asking adolescents questions about the death of a pet? Explain.

2. Was it ethical to administer the ALCES prior to obtaining parental consent? Explain.

3. Would it be a good idea to get parental consent before distributing the "instrument package"? Explain.

---

[1] Source/reference: Brown, B. H., Richards, H. C., & Wilson, C. A. (1996). Pet bonding and pet bereavement among adolescents. *Journal of Counseling and Development, 74,* 505–509.

Case 28

Estimating HIV Rates Among Young Men[1]

Problem: The Center for Disease Control and Prevention (CDC) wanted to estimate the seroprevalence of HIV and risk factors among young men who have sex with men. Their problem was locating an appropriate sample.

A Solution: Working with local health departments, the CDC identified public venues frequented by young men who have sex with men, including dance clubs, bars, parks, street locations, business establishments, and social organizations. At a sample of the venues, one staff member counted the number of young men who appeared to be between 15 and 22 years of age as they entered the area or establishment. Other staff members intercepted the men who were counted and briefly interviewed them to determine if they were eligible for the study.

"Young men who agree to participate are taken to a van parked near the venue. As an added measure to screen out duplicates, recruited men are introduced to all available staff. In the van, trained staff administer a standardized questionnaire to consenting participants, perform HIV/AIDS counseling, draw blood for testing, provide referrals for social support or medical services as needed, and dispense participant stipends.

"Using a standardized questionnaire, staff members conduct confidential face-to-face interviews with young men about their demographic characteristics, venue attendance frequencies, HIV-related risk behaviors, and factors potentially associated with these risk behaviors. In addition to standard demographic items such as age and race/ethnicity, young men are asked about their current household, school, and employment situations, and their parents' educational status."

Your Opinions:

1. Are there ethical problems with soliciting young men as young as age 15 to participate in this study without parental consent? Explain.

2. In addition to collecting research data, the researchers offered services (such as counseling). Does this ameliorate any ethical concerns you have?

3. Suppose the CDC decided to seek parental consent before interviewing the young men. How successful do you think they would be in getting an adequate sample? Explain.

---

[1] Source/reference: MacKellar, D., Valleroy, L., Karon, J., Lemp, G., & Janssen, R. (1996). The Young Men's Survey: Methods for estimating HIV seroprevalence and risk factors among young men who have sex with men. *Public Health Reports*, *111*, 138–144.

Soliciting Professors for a Study of Their Intellect[1]

Problem: Researchers were interested in determining the correlation between professors' age and intellectual ability. Initially, when professors were contacted by telephone to solicit their participation in the study, they were told that the title of the study was "age-related changes and intellectual performance." The researchers found that some of the professors seemed "apprehensive" when informed of this title.

A Solution: "The approach on the telephone was changed in the early stages of the process to a less threatening title of 'age-related changes across the lifespan.'"

Additional Notes: About 74% of the professors contacted by telephone agreed to participate in the study. They were tested individually with a battery of tests "designed to tap fluid intelligence, crystallized intelligence, and memory."

Your Opinions:

1. In your opinion, was it ethical to provide the professors with the more general (less threatening) title instead of the more specific title? Explain.

2. If you had agreed to participate in a study titled "age-related changes across the lifespan," would you have been surprised to find that you were tested for intelligence only while participating in the study? Explain.

3. Speculate on why some professors were apprehensive about the original title. Are there other ways the apprehension could have been alleviated without changing the title? Explain.

4. If some professors refused to participate because of their apprehension, could their refusal bias the study?

5. In your opinion, can the change in the title be justified by the researchers' desire to increase the rate of participation in the study? Explain.

---

[1] Source/reference: Compton, D. M., Bachman, L. D., & Logan, J. A. (1997). Aging and intellectual ability in young, middle-aged, and older educated adults: Preliminary results from a sample of college faculty. *Psychological Reports, 81,* 79–80.

Case 30

Hiding the Purpose of a Study from Employees[1]

Problem: Researchers wanted to test this hypothesis: "Gay and lesbian workers who report a lower extent of communication about sexual orientation…will show less favorable work attitudes than either 'open' homosexuals…or heterosexuals." To test it, they designed a questionnaire that asked about job satisfaction, commitment to the organization for which the respondents worked, as well as the extent to which the gays and lesbians in the study tried to keep their sexual orientation a secret at work.

Since the majority of the respondents were obtained by using a mailing list of a gay and lesbian advocacy organization, the researchers were concerned that some respondents might guess what the hypothesis was while responding to the questionnaire, and because they already believed in the hypothesis, would provide responses consistent with it.

A Solution: "First, we introduced the study only as an 'investigation of work attitudes' whose purpose was to allow us to 'make recommendations to human resource managers regarding effective employment practices that will enhance the productivity of all workers.' The order of the questions was carefully designed so that respondents would be unlikely to anticipate what their answers 'should' be. The questions concerning their sexual orientation and, if they were homosexual, the extent to which they communicated their sexual orientation to coworkers, were not asked until after…" the other questions were asked.

Your Opinions:

1. What is your opinion on introducing the study as a general study of work attitudes instead of introducing it as a study of the work attitudes of different sexual orientation groups? Does this pose any ethical problems?

2. Of the 3,510 questionnaires mailed, only 1,063 usable ones were returned. In your opinion, is it likely that the response rate would have been higher if the introduction to the study for the potential participants had been more specific to the hypothesis (i.e., had explicitly referred to sexual orientation in the introduction)? Explain.

---

[1] Source/reference: Day, N. E., & Schoenrade, P. (1997). Staying in the closet versus coming out: Relationships between communication about sexual orientation and work attitudes. *Personnel Psychology*, *50*, 147–163.

Section I

Short Cases

Part G

Interpretation of Results

Case 31

Interpreting Cause-and-Effect: Health Risk Behaviors of Adolescents[1]

Background: Researchers surveyed older siblings attending college (average age 19) and their younger siblings who were still living at home (average age 15) on a variety of health risk behaviors. Among other things, the researchers found that "The more alcohol younger siblings believed their older siblings drank, the more younger siblings drank."

A Problematic Interpretation: The result is consistent with the proposition that adolescents are *influenced* by the drinking behavior of their older siblings. The researchers state that "…younger siblings may have heard about older sibling drinking when he or she talked about college life. Bravado may lead some older siblings to exaggerate their drinking behavior, which has the unfortunate effect of increasing their younger siblings' alcohol use…"

A Drawback to the Interpretation: The researchers point out that "Parental influence to both groups of siblings was not assessed in the current study. Consequently, younger siblings' drinking behavior and expectancies may partially result from parental influence."

Your Opinions:

1. In your opinion, is the problematic interpretation seriously threatened by the drawback? Explain.

2. Two causal explanations are suggested above (older siblings' influence and parental influence). Are there other possible explanations? Explain.

3. The researchers conducted a nonexperimental study. Would it be possible to conduct an experiment to explore the effects of older siblings' bravado on the drinking behavior of their younger siblings? If yes, explain how it might be done.

4. If you answered "yes" to question 3, would it be ethical to conduct such an experiment?

---

[1] Source/reference: D'Amico, E. J., & Fromme, K. (1997). Health risk behaviors of adolescent and young adult siblings. *Health Psychology*, *16*, 426–432.

Interpreting Results in Light of Social Desirability[1]

Problem: Researchers who were planning to interview adult Hispanics on their awareness of product-warning labels and signs were concerned that some respondents might give socially desirable answers (in this case, it is desirable to be aware of warnings) or may have an acquiescent response set (that is, a tendency to answer in the affirmative to all questions).[2]

A Solution: In addition to asking about warning labels on products such as beer, aspirin, and cigarettes, the researchers also asked respondents to "report if they had seen a warning message on a fruit juice container." Since fruit juice containers do not have warning labels, this was a bogus question.

The percentages who reported being aware of warning labels for some of the products were: beer (31.5%), aspirin (36.7%), cigarettes (69.3%), and fruit juice (8.0%). The researchers stated that social desirability and a motivation to acquiesce "may have been particularly important among the less acculturated Hispanics who were more likely to report awareness of a fictitious product-warning message on fruit juices. [The authors measured acculturation with four questions about language use and preference (at home, work, and with friends) with choices that range from 'mostly English' to 'mostly Spanish.'] It should be pointed out, nevertheless, that reports of the existence of fictitious product warning messages have also been found [in another study] among non-Hispanics in proportions similar to those reported in this paper. If the level of awareness of this bogus message were subtracted as a 'correction factor' of the reported awareness of the actual warning messages, the data would show a yet lower level of awareness of the messages."

Your Opinions:

1. Was it a good idea to include a bogus item on fruit juice? Does it make sense that the less acculturated were more likely to answer in the affirmative to this item? Explain.

2. Do you think it would be a good idea to use the 8% as a correction factor when estimating the respondents' awareness of warning labels [for example, for beer using 23.5% (31.5% minus 8.0%) as a more accurate estimate than 31.5%]?

---

[1] Source/reference: Marín, G. (1994). Self-reported awareness of the presence of product warning messages and signs by Hispanics in San Francisco. *Public Health Reports, 109*, 275–283.
[2] Additional information on this study can be found in Case 1.

Case 33

Evaluating Attrition in a Study on Hypnosis[1]

Problem: Some participants may drop out during the course of a study. In research, this is known as *attrition*. Attrition is a problem because those who drop out may be systematically different from those who remain.

In a study on the effects of hypnosis on relieving public speaking anxiety, 62 men and women were assigned to one of three groups: (1) an experimental group that received hypnosis as well as cognitive behavioral therapy that included hypnotic suggestions, (2) a comparison group that received the cognitive behavioral therapy without hypnotic suggestions, or (3) a control group that received no treatment. The design called for all participants in all groups to be pretested and posttested by having them give an impromptu speech on an assigned topic and rating their own anxiety while giving the speech.

Two of those in the experimental group and three of those in the control group refused to give a pretreatment speech (i.e., the pretest). Although all control group "participants were offered treatment at the end of the 5-week [treatment] period, many said they were no longer interested in treatment at that time and also expressed reluctance to return for the posttreatment assessment session [i.e., the posttest]. In order to increase the number of completers in the control condition, those expressing reluctance were offered $5.00 for their participation. Four of the 10 people in the control group who participated in posttreatment assessment were paid; 11 people in the control group did not return for posttreatment assessment."

Your Opinions:

1. In your opinion, were the five participants who refused to give the pretreatment speech likely to be more or less anxious about public speaking than those who gave the speech? Could this affect the results of the study? Explain.

2. Ten of the 21 participants in the control group did not take the posttest. Does this pose problems for the interpretation of the results? Explain.

3. What is your opinion on giving four people in the control group $5.00 to return for posttesting? Could it affect the outcome study? Do you think the researchers should have offered a larger amount in order to get a larger number to return?

---

[1] Source/reference: Schoenberger, N. E., Kirsch, I., Gearan, P., Montgomery, G., & Pastyrnak, S. L. (1997). Hypnotic enhancement of a cognitive behavioral treatment for public speaking anxiety. *Behavior Therapy*, *28*, 127–140.

Case 34

Interpreting Differences in Physical Victimization[1]

Problem: Researchers conducted face-to-face interviews with 1,978 individuals in the United Kingdom who were involved in heterosexual relationships. They asked participants to respond to items about physical victimization such as "Your partner has slapped you (you have slapped your partner)" and "Your partner has punched or kicked you (you have punched or kicked your partner)." Among other things, they found that younger respondents reported more victimization across all their relationships than older respondents. For example, in the 15- to 34-year age group, 21% of the women reported at least one act of victimization across all relationships; only 12% of the women in the 35 to 54 age group reported this, and only 7% of the women aged 55 and over did so. The researchers state that "a clear inference drawn from these results is that victimization of women by male partners is more likely for women who are…young" than those who are older.

An Interpretation. "It can also be suggested that there is some evidence to suggest that assaults between partners in the United Kingdom is increasing, given the higher percentage of incidence in the youngest age group."

Your Opinions:

1. The interpretation refers to changes across time (i.e., across time, victimization appears to be increasing). One way to study changes across time is with a *longitudinal study* in which participants' behavior is tracked across time to measure changes. The study reported here is *cross sectional* in which cross sections of different age groups are compared at one point in time. In your opinion, which type of study is better for determining whether assaults are increasing? Explain.

2. All the women were asked to recall victimization during all relationships in their lifetimes. However, for the older women, this task requires recollection across a very long time span. In your opinion, is this a serious problem? Does it affect your interpretation of the data? Explain.

---

[1] Source/reference: Carrado, M., George, M. J., Loxam, E., Jones, L., & Templar, D. (1996). Aggresssion in British heterosexual relationships: A descriptive analysis. *Aggressive Behavior, 22,* 401–415.

Interpreting Reported Differences in Husbands' Marital Aggression[1]

Problem: Researchers wanted to study husbands' marital aggression by interviewing young couples at the time they were married and again one year later. Individual interviews were to be conducted at the institute where the research was being conducted. Some lived too far to come to the institute and some refused to come to the institute or failed to keep their appointments, even though repeated appointments were made.

A Solution: Those who could not be interviewed in person at the institute (34% of the sample) were interviewed by phone.

Results and an Interpretation: "Couples interviewed in person were more likely to report wife employment...and a current pregnancy... Couples who were interviewed by phone reported significantly lower levels of marital aggression...than did persons interviewed in person. A...limitation concerns the necessity of using telephone interviews and the lower rate of marital aggression observed in these couples. These results suggest that more valid reports of marital aggression could be achieved through the use of face-to-face as opposed to phone interviews. Given that many influential studies of marital aggression have been conducted with phone interviews, the implications of this finding for future studies are considerable."

Your Opinions:

1. In your opinion, are those who refuse to return to the institute to be interviewed more likely or less likely to have marriages with serious husband aggression? Explain.

2. Do you agree with the researchers' interpretation that the face-to-face interview data is more valid than the telephone data? Explain.

3. If you answered yes to question 2, was it still worthwhile to collect the telephone data? Explain.

---

[1] Source/reference: Leonard, K. E., Senchak, M. (1996). Prospective prediction of husband marital aggression within newlywed couples. *Journal of Abnormal Psychology, 105*, 369–380. Copyright © 1996 by the American Psychological Association, Inc.

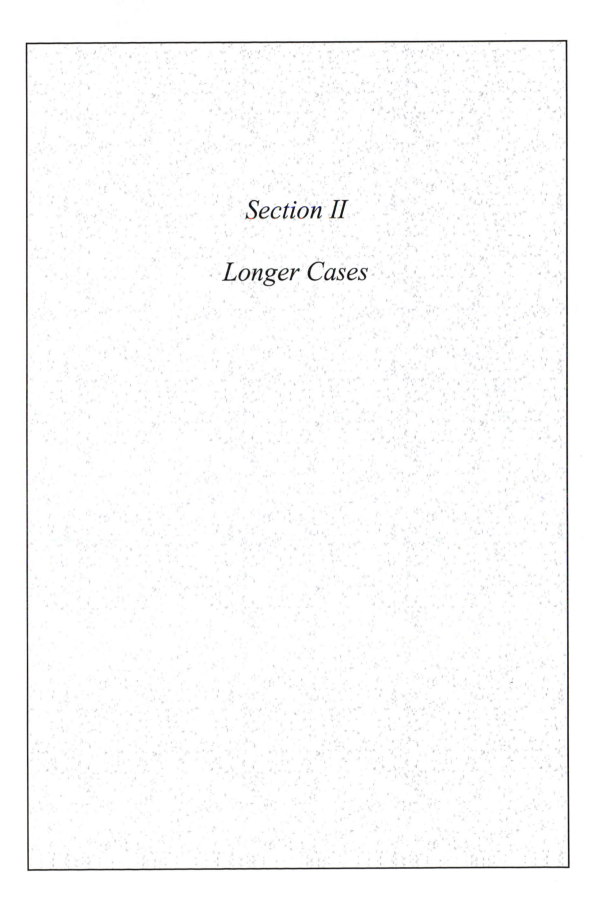

Section II

Longer Cases

Notes:

Case 36

Using Interviews to Measure Mothers' Use of Physical Discipline[1]

Problem: Researchers wanted to study mothers' use of physical discipline by having research assistants interview mothers. To do this, the researchers needed to develop an interview protocol for the assistants to follow.

A Solution: "Our aim in the maternal interview was to assess the overall discipline experience of the child; this was done by conducting a detailed, open-ended interview, followed by a summary rating made by the trained researcher. This format was used because it allowed parents to describe their discipline strategies in their own words, and it also enabled the interviewer to be culturally sensitive when assessing each mother's description.

"During the interview, the mother answered several questions regarding the discipline of the child: Who usually disciplined the child? How was the child disciplined? Was the child ever punished physically? If physical punishment was used, how did adults usually spank the child (e.g., with the hand or with objects)? After hearing answers to these questions, the interviewer coded parents' responses on a 5-point scale, rating the degree of physical discipline received by the child. Scores were coded using the following three anchor points: 1 (nonrestrictive, mostly positive guidance), 3 (moderately restrictive, sometimes physical), and 5 (severe, strict, often physical). All interviewers attained interrater reliability of .80 or higher (compared with a criterion interviewer's responses) in practice interviews before conducting participant interviews. In addition, two research assistants conducted the in-home interviews for 56 randomly selected families [out of a total of 578 families interviewed in this study]; interrater agreement was good ($r = .80$). On average, mothers ($n = 578$) reported moderately harsh discipline ($M = 2.60$, $SD = 0.96$, range = 1 to 5).

"Toward the end of the in-home interview, the researcher administered the structured concerns and constraints interview. This measure includes the presentation of five hypothetical vignettes involving child misbehavior: (a) child losing a race and calling the winner a bad name, (b) pushing a peer after being accidentally bumped, (c) threatening to throw a ball into the sewer if peers do not let him or her join in a game, (d) intentionally not inviting a cousin to his or her birthday party and talking back when asked why, and (e) teasing a peer by saying he or she is dumb. After each vignette had been described to the mother, she was

---

[1] Source/reference: Deater-Deckard, K., Dodge, K. A., Bates, J. E., & Pettit, G. S. (1996). Physical discipline among African American and European American mothers: Links to children's externalizing behaviors. *Developmental Psychology*, *32*, 1065–1072. Copyright © 1996 by the American Psychological Association, Inc. Reprinted with permission.

45

asked several questions about why she thought the child had behaved this way, how she would feel if her child behaved this way, and what she would do if her child behaved this way. The mother's free response was coded as to whether it involved the use of physical punishment (including spanking and hitting); a score of 1 was given if physical punishment was reported, and a score of 0 was given if it was not reported. A total physical punishment score was computed by averaging across the five vignettes ($n = 552$, $M = .06$, $SD = .13$, range = .00 to .80)…so that higher scores corresponded with greater use of physical punishment."

Your Opinions:

1. Speculate on what the researchers mean by "open-ended interview." How do you think it differs from a "closed-ended interview"? Explain.

2. Are there advantages and disadvantages to using open-ended interviews? Explain.

3. Speculate on what the researchers mean by "criterion interviewer."

4. Speculate on why only 56 of the 578 mothers were interviewed by two research assistants, while the rest were interviewed by only one assistant.

5. Do you agree that $r = .80$ indicates good interrater reliability? If you have a research methods textbook that describes interrater reliability, does the textbook author suggest any standards for judging its adequacy? If yes, write your findings here.

6. The interviews were conducted in the family's homes. What are some reasons why a researcher might prefer to conduct the interviews in the homes? What are some reasons why he or she might prefer to conduct the interviews someplace other than the homes?

7. First, the mothers were interviewed on how they disciplined their own children. This was followed by a "concerns and constraints" interview that asked about children's hypothetical behavior. Speculate on why the researchers used the concerns and constraints interview given that they already had information on how the mothers actually disciplined their own children.

8. For the concerns and constraints interview, the researchers report a mean (M) of .06. Does this indicate that the average mother leaned more toward giving physical punishment *or* more toward not giving physical punishment in the hypothetical situations?

9. All the hypothetical vignettes involve relatively minor child misbehaviors (e.g., teasing a peer). Should more serious ones (e.g., stealing) have been included? If yes, would their inclusion yield more valid information? Would it change the nature of the study? Explain.

10. In addition to using interviews, are there alternative methods for gathering data on mothers' use of physical discipline? Are the alternatives as good as the interview method? Explain.

Notes:

Case 37

Defining Group Therapy Used with Elementary School Children[1]

Problem: In experiments, researchers give treatments, which need to be described in sufficient detail so that readers get a good idea of the nature of the treatments. In addition, research methods textbooks also suggest that treatments should be *operationally defined*, that is, defined in terms of specific physical steps. Operational definitions allow consumers of research to implement the treatments in their own settings. In addition, they allow other researchers to replicate the results by using exactly the same treatments in additional studies. Thus, there are two standards by which the description of a treatment used in an experiment may be judged: (1) does it give readers a "good idea" of the general nature of the treatment, and (2) does it define the treatment operationally.

A problem researchers face when writing for journals is that journal space is limited, which often limits the length of the descriptions of the treatments used in experiments.

The Description of a Treatment Used in an Experiment: Researchers reported on the effects of 20 45-minute weekly group therapy sessions with low achievers in elementary school. The results suggested that the therapy was successful in improving academic achievement, self-concept, social acceptance, and students' personal responsibility for school performance. The treatment was described in a six-page journal article as follows:

"Interactional group therapy, which is generally used with adults, was adjusted to meet the needs of elementary school children. The focus was on facilitating self-expression and listening skills through structured activities, therapeutic games, bibliotherapy, and art therapy, as recommended by experts in the field (Cramer-Azima, 1995) Notwithstanding these modifications, the process emphasized the major therapeutic factors identified as effective in therapy groups. In an effort to promote group cohesiveness, the initial sessions were largely structured and aimed at enhancing interpersonal acquaintance by breaking the ice. At this stage, children told about the origins of their names, shared positive aspects of self and personal gains, and participated in group projects involving building blocks and artwork. Next, stories, art, cards, and games were used to extend the language of feelings and to set the norm for self-expression. Thereafter, issues of

---

[1] Source/reference: Shechtman, Z., Gilat, I., Fos, L., & Flasher, A. (1996). Brief group therapy with low-achieving elementary school children. *Journal of Counseling Psychology*, *43*, 376-382. Copyright © 1996 by the American Psychological Association, Inc. Reprinted with permission.

trust emerged, and some rules and regulations were established for the group, with a strong focus on confidentiality.

"Although the activities and supportive devices included in the treatment may resemble ongoing work of other groups in the school, the strong emotional and experiential components were what characterized this experience. In general, after resolving the storming stage of group development, the children started to set goals for their participation, voluntarily introducing to the group problems with peers, self, and family. Often, conflictual group relationships and behavior surfaced and were handled with empathy and sensitivity. It was the counselor's task to lead the group to respond in this manner, either through modeling or through skill training. Members were strongly encouraged to share similar feelings and experiences—that is, not merely to provide support but also to be actively involved. Often role-playing or a clarifying process was used to enhance feelings of personal responsibility and to facilitate change.

"Because the group therapy process was nonstructured, a manual was not required. However, the similar background in training and supervision of the counselors largely guaranteed the similarity of the interventions across groups. All the structured activities were drawn from the same repertoire of activities, and the group process followed a similar format.

"The treatment groups were led by three female school counselors with varying levels of experience in group therapy… One group leader was a highly experienced group therapist, and the other two were experienced school teachers but novices in leading therapy groups. All three, who are co-authors in this study, received their training in group counseling from Zipora Shechtman [the veteran therapist, who was the lead author of the journal article in which this research is reported]. Moreover, the novice group therapists interned with the veteran counselor before the study and remained under her supervision during the course of the intervention. This helped to ensure that the group process was relatively uniform, regardless of the leader."

Your Opinions:

1. To what extent does the description of the treatment give the reader a good idea of the general nature of the treatment?

2. Here is one aspect of the treatment that was highly operationalized: There were 20 weekly group therapy sessions lasting 45 minutes each. If you were replicating this study, you would know exactly how many sessions to schedule, how often to schedule them (weekly) and how long each should last. In your opinion, are any other aspects of the treatment highly operationalized?

3. Given that the researchers deliberately decided to use "nonstructured" group therapy, is it necessary and/or desirable to provide an operational definition of the therapy? Is there a logical problem with expecting the researchers to provide an operational definition of an *unstructured* treatment? (Note: Specifying exactly what a therapist should do and say would "structure" the therapy, which would change the nature of the variable that the researchers wanted to study.)

4. In the conclusion to their journal article (not shown here), the researchers state that "In future research, investigators should compare the methods used in this study with other available types of treatment to establish their credibility as a chosen intervention. It would be particularly interesting to compare interactional group therapy with cognition- and behavior-oriented treatments…" In your opinion, would future research be facilitated if highly operational definitions of the three types of therapy were developed and used to guide the research? Explain.

5. One way researchers help readers obtain an operational definition of the treatment used in their experiments is to refer the readers to other, more detailed published sources of information on the treatments. In the excerpt shown above, the researchers refer readers to Cramer-Azima (1995), which has this reference: "*Working with children and adolescents in group therapy*. Workshop presented at the National Group Therapists Network, Ramat-Gan, Israel." In your opinion, would additional references be helpful? Explain.

6. In your opinion, is there a danger that the results obtained in this study might not generalize to group therapy when led by other therapists who were not trained in group processes by the lead author of the research? Explain.

7. If you had been a reviewer of articles being considered for possible publication in the journal in which this study was published, would you have suggested that a more operational definition be incorporated into the article before acceptance for publication? If yes, what specific guidance would you have given to guide the researchers in revising their description?

Notes:

Getting Informed Consent for Research During an Emergency[1]

Problem: Researchers wanted to compare two treatments for newborn infants who had acute respiratory failure: a conventional treatment (CM) and a new treatment known as ECMO. The design of the study called for random assignment of each baby to one of the treatment conditions, which was referred to by the researchers as a *randomized controlled trial*. Such a study is also known in research circles as a *true experiment*.

"The 'experimental' treatment, ECMO, has been widely adopted elsewhere, despite the lack of unbiased evidence about its effectiveness. The three North American trials...which have attempted to consider this question are extremely difficult to interpret because of the unorthodox design of the first two, and the small sample sizes of all three... [This United Kingdom (U.K.) trial] aimed to provide clear evidence of the role of ECMO in neonatal intensive care before it was generally adopted into clinical practice. Crucially, the trial aimed to assess not only initial survival but also outcome at one year. In this way the possibility of increased rates of survival with increased rates of disability could be considered.

"As an unevaluated treatment...ECMO was not available outside the trial in the U.K. The only means of possible access to ECMO was therefore to consent to the trial and random allocation of treatment.

"Recruitment to the ECMO trial took place...in over 80 participating centres. Parents were given letters and information leaflets prepared by the...steering committee (which included lay members). These may be obtained from the second author. Oral rather than written consent was required for the trial. Some centres were required by local research ethics committees to amend or replace the...documentation and in some instances to use their own consent forms. The basic information given to parents was therefore not uniform and any additional information given was dependent upon departmental policy and the recruiting clinician. Clinicians were asked to inform parents [about the trial] and to expand on the written information. The actual exchange was left to the judgement of individual clinicians and was not otherwise monitored. The trial involved 185 babies in total, of whom 101 survived to one year of age, and 84 died."

At the end of the study, researchers used a questionnaire and interviews with a sample of the parents to determine the circumstances under which they gave consent as well as their understanding of the randomization process that was

---

[1] Source/reference: Reprinted from Snowdon, C., Garcia, J., & Elbourne, D. (1997). Making sense of randomization: Responses of parents of critically ill babies to random allocation of treatment in a clinical trial. *Social Science & Medicine, 45*, 1337–1355. Copyright © 1997 with permission from Elsevier Science.

used to assign treatments. The researchers found that "In each interview it was clear that parents had been asked to consider the trial at a time of great stress and sometimes confusion. In some cases babies were taken straight from the delivery room for intensive care with little or no time for parental contact. As the condition of these babies often deteriorated rapidly, many were receiving 100% supplemental oxygen on a ventilator only hours after birth. This was particularly unexpected for parents after a full-term pregnancy. They were often left in no doubt that their baby's life was in danger. Some were given Polaroid photographs and, for most, staff had raised the subject of a baptism.

"The entry criteria for the trial involved a very severe level of illness. Parents were approached only when the baby deteriorated sufficiently to meet those requirements. The high chance of death in all cases meant that discussions could not be delayed. Fathers who had gone home to sleep were asked to return to the hospital to discuss the trial in the knowledge of the worsening condition of the baby. All women had very recently given birth; some had had a planned or emergency Caesarian section, some involving a general anaesthetic. Some were approached during the night for consent, and two women had to be woken after they had taken sleeping drugs. In spite of these difficult circumstances, the majority of parents were required to make a relatively speedy decision. They were not able to take time to absorb information about the trial over a number of days and decide when they were comfortable, as time was simply not available. It is in this context that worried and exhausted parents had to take on board not only a quantity of information but grasp the rather strange concept of randomization."

In addition, the researchers found that some of the parents misunderstood or only partially understood the random process as it applied to their babies' treatment. For example, some parents thought that the treatment decision was deliberately made by physicians based on what the physicians thought was to be best for their babies. Some parents whose babies received ECMO thought that they had chosen it when, in reality, their babies had been assigned at random to the treatment. Still others were concerned or angry that randomization was used to determine treatment.

Some Solutions: An alternative in situations like these is the "Zelen approach" (named for the researcher who suggested it). "In this method, randomization takes place before potential participants are approached. Only those allocated to the experimental therapies are informed of a trial and invited to give or withhold consent. Those allocated to continue with standard therapies are not informed that they are trial participants at that stage." A second approach is to administer "a brief questionnaire after a consent form has been read [but not yet signed] to test understanding of key issues such as the purpose of the trial and potential risks involved." Misunderstanding can then be addressed before consent is given. A third approach is to tape record conversations between participants and researchers concerning the trial; participants can then listen to the details as often as they wish in order to gain a fuller understanding.

Your Opinions:

1. If you had planned the informed consent procedure, would you have relied on oral consent? Explain.

2. Do you think it was a good idea to allow clinicians to expand on the written consent information and enter into a verbal exchange with parents without a prepared script? Explain.

3. The study was referred to as a "randomized trial" when getting consent from parents. In your opinion, would it have been better to refer to it as a "randomized experiment"? Explain.

4. The researchers refer to the "strange concept of randomization." How would you have explained it to parents so that it seemed less strange?

5. What is your opinion of the Zelen approach? Are there any drawbacks to it?

6. What is your opinion on using a questionnaire to test for parents' understanding of the consent form before they sign it?

7. Do you think it would be a good idea to tape-record the discussions of the trial for parents to listen to as often as they want? Explain.

8. If you were a parent who had this experience, would you have been angry that randomization was used to select a treatment for your baby? If yes, is there anything else the researchers could have done to ameliorate your anger? Explain.

9. To justify clinical trials of the type presented here, some researchers suggest that the experimental treatment must be sufficiently promising to warrant its experimental use, but must also be sufficiently in question as to its efficacy and side effects to warrant withholding it from a control group. Does this seem to be the case in the clinical trial discussed above? Explain.

Notes:

Case 39

Interpreting Data on Cigarette Smoking by Seventh Graders[1]

Problem: Researchers would like to examine the extent to which cigarette advertising *causes* adolescents to smoke. For ethical and legal reasons, a true experiment in which a random half of a sample of adolescents is exposed to cigarette advertising by the researchers cannot be conducted. Instead, they rely on descriptive data on the relationship between advertising and smoking. The descriptive nature of the data means that any interpretations regarding causality must be tentative.

Below, researchers summarize and interpret the results they found by surveying seventh graders in San Jose, California on their exposure to various types of cigarette advertising and their smoking behavior.

Summary of Results and Interpretation: Because the number of students who were regular smokers was small, the analysis focused on the relationship between *experimentation* with smoking and exposure to tobacco marketing. "Forty-one percent of participants reported having experimented with cigarettes; this was defined as ever having tried cigarette smoking, even if just a puff.

"Results of our school-based survey of 571 ethnically and socioeconomically diverse seventh graders reveal that 88% reported exposure to tobacco marketing. Adolescents are exposed to cigarette advertising and promotions in magazines, on billboards, through the mail, in stores, at sports and community events—indeed, in various ways as they travel to and from school, go shopping, and engage in other daily activities. These data paint a compelling picture of youth environments that are saturated with pro-smoking cues and messages.

"These high levels of exposure to tobacco marketing are troubling because of their relationship to students' smoking behavior. Our results indicate that perceived exposure to tobacco advertising and promotion is associated with self-reported tobacco use even when we controlled for the powerful influences of friends and family. [This was controlled for statistically in the analysis of the data.] In fact, it appears that exposure to cigarette marketing is a more important predictor of youth's experimentation with cigarettes than is parental or sibling smoking. In addition, our data suggest that marketing materials may shape young people's attitudes. Participants reported that they were most likely to own items

---

[1] Source/reference: Schooler, C., Feighery, E., & Flora, J. A. (1996). Seventh graders' self-reported exposure to cigarette marketing and its relationship to their smoking behavior. *American Journal of Public Health, 86,* 1216-1221. Copyright © American Public Health Association. Reprinted by permission.

and receive mail from Marlboro and Camel, had favorite ads for these brands, and were more likely to have experimented with and to want these brands. These data corroborate previous research demonstrating youth preferences for heavily advertised brands of cigarettes…

"Our data are unique in that we examine the wide array of advertising and promotions to which young people are exposed. Our analyses suggest that those who receive mailings [such as surveys, coupons, free gifts, product catalogs, or free cigarettes addressed to them from cigarette companies] are almost three times as likely to experiment with cigarettes, and youth who own [cigarette] promotional items [such as lighters and T-shirts] are more than twice as likely to smoke. Exposure to in-store cigarette marketing [banners, posters, and signs promoting cigarettes] increases the chance a young person will smoke by almost 40%…

"This sample includes only two school districts in Northern California and is more heavily minority (particularly Asian) than the US population as a whole. However, because the smoking rates we report (41% experimenters, 9% current smokers) are comparable to those reported in other national…and California…studies, the generalizability of these data may not be as limited as they might first seem. Another potential limitation of this study is our reliance on self-reported data, raising the possibility of response bias. The substantial variance in reported smoking behavior, ranging from 41% reporting experimenting to 4% reporting daily smoking suggests that respondents were truthful. Moreover, responses to behavioral items [i.e., questions on smoking behavior] reliably discriminated between levels of perceived exposure. The fact that our findings are consistent with previous research and the logical gradation of responses provides confidence regarding the accuracy of these data. Although this is a cross-sectional survey and we are thus unable to draw causal inferences regarding the effects of cigarette advertising and promotion, our findings are highly complementary with other published work. We feel, therefore, that these results support previous research suggesting a causal connection between cigarette marketing and consumption…"

Your Opinions:

1. Should the interpretation of the results be tempered by the fact that the researchers examined experimenting with cigarettes instead of smoking behavior? Explain.

2. The researchers report that 88% of the sample reported exposure to tobacco marketing. If you were interpreting this result, would you call it "surprising"? Explain.

3. The researchers report that those who own cigarette promotional items are more than twice as likely to smoke than those who do not own them. Is this direct evidence that cigarette promotional items cause adolescents to smoke? Explain.

4. The researchers report that exposure to in-store cigarette marketing *increases* the chance that a young person will smoke by almost 40%. Is it also possible that smoking by young people *increases* the chance that they will frequent stores with in-store cigarette marketing? If yes, could both interpretations be correct (that is, one interpretation is correct for some adolescents and the other interpretation is correct for other adolescents)? Explain.

5. In your opinion, how limiting is the fact that only two school districts were surveyed and that they were more heavily minority than the U.S. population as a whole?

6. Do you agree with the authors' interpretation that the substantial variance in reported smoking behavior is evidence that the respondents were truthful? Explain.

7. Do you agree with the authors that their results *only support* other research suggesting a causal connection rather than providing direct evidence on a causal connection?

8. The researchers note that their survey is *cross-sectional*; by this, they mean that they measured exposure to advertising and smoking behavior *at the same time*. An alternative is a longitudinal prospective study in which children who initially do not smoke are studied over time to determine their exposure to cigarette advertising. A researcher could then determine whether more of those who had greater exposure to advertising eventually ended up smoking. In your opinion, would a prospective study provide better evidence of a causal link? If yes, explain why.

9. Would a longitudinal prospective study be as good for establishing causality as a true experiment with random assignment to different levels of exposure to cigarette advertising (with researchers observing smoking behavior subsequent to the exposure)? Explain.

Notes:

Case 40

Encouraging Responses to a Mailed Survey[1]

Problem: Normally, nonrespondents to a mailed survey are presumed to bias the results of a study because they may systematically differ from the respondents. For example, those who are more interested in the topic of a questionnaire may be more likely to return it than those who are less interested; furthermore, those who are more interested may hold different opinions than those who are less interested.

Follow-up mailings to nonrespondents usually result in an increased response rate. However, if questionnaires are anonymous, researchers do not know which of the potential respondents to contact with follow-up mailings. One solution is to send a follow-up mailing to all potential respondents with instructions to ignore the follow-up mailing if they have already mailed their questionnaires back. Other solutions to this problem were used in a survey on controversial issues in using polygraph (lie detector) tests; these solutions are described below.

Research Methods: To encourage respondents to return the questionnaires, the researchers kept the questionnaires short "limiting the surveys to a cover letter with three pages of questions and sending follow-up prompts to those slow in responding."

Two groups were mailed questionnaires. The first group consisted of the Society for Psychophysiological Research (SPR). "The SPR survey was mailed…along with a stamped return envelope and reply card [that identified them] that respondents were asked to mail under separate cover after they had mailed their survey. In this way, anonymity was assured while making it possible to track respondents. Within about 2 weeks of this mailing, a postcard was sent to prompt responding. About 3 weeks after the initial mailing, nonresponders were sent a second survey with return envelopes and postcards. Approximately 7 weeks after the initial mailing, this process was repeated, with nonresponders receiving a personalized note exhorting them to complete the survey."

The second group consisted of all Fellows (full members) of Division 1 (General Psychology) of the American Psychological Association (APA). "We sent Fellows a letter alerting them to our intention to mail them a survey on lie detection. Two weeks later, we mailed the surveys along with a dollar bill and a stamped return envelope. Rather than enclose a postcard for tracking respondents, surveys were marked with an identification number for tracking purposes, and respondents were promised confidentiality. Follow-up mailings, including another

---

[1] Source/reference: Iacono, W. G., & Lykken, D. T. (1997). The validity of the lie detector: Two surveys of scientific opinion, *Journal of Applied Psychology 82*, 426–433. Copyright © 1997 by the American Psychological Association, Inc. Reprinted by permission.

survey and stamped envelope, were sent to nonresponders about 1 and 2 months after the initial contact letter.

"Of the surveys sent to 216 SPR members, two were returned as nondeliverable. Of the 214 remaining, 195 members (91%) returned questionnaires. The average age of the respondents, of whom 79% were men and 21% were women, was 47 years ($SD = 10.8$).

"In the case of the APA Fellows, 249 surveys were mailed. Nine of these were returned as nondeliverable, and communications were received from an additional 14 indicating that the APA member was either now deceased or unable to respond for health reasons. Of the 226 remaining, 168…or 74% returned usable questionnaires. … The sample consisted of 84% men and 16% women. The average age of respondents was 64 years ($SD = 11.1$). It was possible to use an APA biographical directory to determine whether those who did not respond to the survey differed in age or sex from the responders. The average age of the nonresponders was 66 years ($SD = 12.3$). Of the 59 nonresponders, 50 (85%) were men. Hence, the age and the sex of the nonresponders were quite similar to that of the responders.

"Both surveys…elicited healthy return rates for mailed questionnaires."

Your Opinions:

1. The researchers sent a dollar bill with the questionnaires that they sent to the APA Fellows. Is this a sufficient amount to compensate the Fellows for their effort in completing the questionnaire? If no, speculate on why the dollar was enclosed.

2. The APA Fellows were first sent a letter telling them that a questionnaire would be mailed to them. Does this seem like a good idea? Why? Why not?

3. The SPR group was asked to mail a reply card separately so that the respondents could be identified. For the APA group, the questionnaires were marked with an identification number, with confidentiality assured. Speculate on the advantages and disadvantages of each method. If you had to use one of these methods for identifying respondents, which one would you use?

4. The response rate for the SPR group was 91%, while the response rate for the APA group was 74%. Is it possible to determine whether this response rate is attributable to the differences in techniques used to identify respondents (i.e., reply cards versus identification numbers on questionnaires)? Explain.

5. Since the researchers were both professors at the University of Minnesota, the cover letter might have been written on University of Minnesota letterhead stationery. If so, do you think this might increase the confidence of the respondents that the research was a legitimate scientific survey? Might it increase confidence that the responses would be kept confidential?

6. If you were sent a survey consisting of a cover letter and three pages of questions, would you consider it to be a short questionnaire? Are you more likely to respond to a short questionnaire than a long one? Explain.

7. Two of the questionnaires sent to the SPR group and nine of the ones sent to the APA group were nondeliverable. Is this a problem? Could it bias the results of the study?

8. The authors were able to determine that the APA responders and nonresponders were similar in age and sex. Is this important? Does this assure you that they were similar in other important respects? Explain.

9. Some members of both groups were contacted a total of four times. Does this surprise you? If you had planned this study, would you have planned to have up to four contacts to increase the response rate? Explain.

10. Do you agree that the researchers obtained "healthy response rates" considering that they were using mailed questionnaires? Explain.

Notes:

Case 41

Interpreting Limitations in a Study of Childhood Cancer and Stress[1]

Problem: Researchers wanted to assess posttraumatic stress symptoms in children and adolescents who were survivors of cancer. Families of survivors who had been off treatment for at least one year were contacted by mail and phone. Ninety-one percent of the families contacted agreed to participate in the study, but only 62% of these families returned the questionnaires that were mailed to them. Near the end of their research report, the researchers discussed this and other problems that are described below.

Limitations: "Although this is the largest study of this type, there are some limitations that should be noted. Childhood cancer patients have been noted to commonly use denial as a coping style. If so, the number of symptoms reported by the survivors would be an underestimate. Assessment using observation, other reporters, or physiological data may be needed to get a more complete view of symptoms in this population. Although childhood cancer is a significant stressor, it would be considered a moderate-level traumatic event, more comparable, for example, to living in a neighborhood plagued by gang violence than to being in a concentration camp. It may be that the...[results we have obtained apply to] children exposed to comparable events, such as diagnosis with other life-threatening illnesses requiring chronic, intrusive treatment, but is less applicable to the children commonly seen by pediatricians after acute, horrifying events, such as motor vehicle accidents or interpersonal violence. Care must be taken not to generalize these findings beyond circumstances comparable to those of survivors of childhood cancer.

"Another limitation to the generalizability of our findings is the fact that this study was conducted in English. Although the ethnic and racial distribution of the patients is generally consistent with the population seen for treatment at the two hospitals, a substantial minority (approximately 25%) of patients seen at the West Coast site were excluded because they were monolingual Spanish speaking. Plans are underway to pilot a similar study, with appropriate revision for culture, with the Spanish-speaking population at [this site]...

"A concern about this study is the self-selection of participants as a threat to the generalizability of the findings. Although 91% of those families located and contacted agreed to participate, only 246 of 398 packets sent were completed and

---

[1] Source/reference: Stuber, M. L., Kazak, A. E., Meeske, K., Barakat, L., Guthrie, D., Garnier, H., Pynoos, R., & Meadows, A. (1997). Predictors of Posttraumatic Stress Symptoms in Childhood Cancer Survivors. *Pediatrics*, *100*, 958–963. Reproduced by permission of Pediatrics.

returned. Parents who gave reasons for nonparticipation reported that the questionnaires were seen as upsetting or irrelevant. Some parents stated that they did not want their children to think about the events again. This may reflect the parental wish to avoid reminders more than…[the children's wish to avoid them]. However, this type of self-selection could bias the results. Although the participants and nonparticipants did not differ when compared on the variables that could be obtained from the tumor registry (gender, diagnosis, age at diagnosis, time off treatment, time on treatment, or intensity of treatment), these factors were generally not those that seemed to predict severity of posttraumatic stress symptoms. It may be that the data represent a significant underestimate of symptoms, if the most symptomatic survivors and parents systematically refused to participate. A case has been made for this interpretation of the nonparticipants in a recent study of 40 adolescents and young adults who were survivors of childhood cancer. Evaluation of self-reports found a significant association between denial of distress and higher levels of intrusive memories and avoidance, which are symptoms of posttraumatic stress syndrome (PTSD). [These] authors make the case that the large number of potential patients who agreed to participate, but never completed the [questionnaires in the current study], reflected those who were most in need of avoidance of reminders, and therefore likely to be the most distressed.

"The further reductions of the sample were done for statistical reasons, and are less problematic. The reduction from 246 to 222 was the result of dropping the youngest children, as a preliminary review of the data suggested that the 7-year-old children were not understanding some of the questions. The further reduction of the sample from 222 to 186 in the path analysis [a statistical technique that requires complete data for all participants in order to be used properly] reflects the number of children without any missing data, because children (or their mothers) who fail to complete any measure are dropped from this type of analysis.

"It is important to note, however, that the majority of survivors reported a mild level of posttraumatic stress symptoms. Although severe posttraumatic stress symptoms can be very disruptive to normal functioning and development, mild symptoms might in some cases be advantageous and appropriate for cancer survivors. Vigilance that is directed toward careful health care and follow-up of problems may have a survival function for these young people, given their increased risk for various long-term complications. Reminders may serve to keep survivors from engaging in high-risk behaviors, such as smoking. Thus, our findings do not necessarily mean that the survivors' responses are pathological. We have collected interview data on a subset of survivors and mothers to understand more about the types of symptoms reported and their potential implications for functioning and health care. We are also analyzing data from the survivors who reported severe levels of symptoms to see if they differ in any significant ways from those in the moderate or mild range."

Your Opinions:

1. The researchers note that their study is "the largest study of this type." In your opinion, is this fact important? Is it as important as whether the sample is biased? Explain.

2. The researchers suggest that the results of this study might be generalized to children with "other life-threatening illnesses." Do you agree? Explain.

3. About 25% of the parents at the West Coast site were excluded because they were monolingual Spanish speakers. In your opinion, is this an important limitation of the study?

4. To determine their interest in participating, parents were "sent a letter describing the study's goal to assess medical and psychological adjustment of cancer survivors. Follow-up phone calls were made to the families to answer [their] questions [about the study] and to determine their interest in participation." While 91% of the parents agreed to participate, only 62% mailed back the questionnaires. Does this surprise you? Explain.

5. Parents who agreed on the phone to participate were mailed the following instruments: a 20-item posttraumatic stress reaction questionnaire, a 37-item true-false anxiety scale, a 17-item questionnaire measuring social support, a 7-item questionnaire on how serious the cancer was from the participants' perspective, and a 27-item questionnaire on stressful events other than cancer experienced by the participants. In your opinion, could the number and length of the questionnaires have affected the response rate in this study? Explain.

6. In the next to the last paragraph shown above, the researchers state that thirty-six (222 minus 186) families were dropped from the sample because they failed to complete one or more of the questionnaires. Do you agree that this loss of subjects is "less problematic" than the loss caused by families failing to return the questionnaires? Explain.

7. Would you be more interested in knowing the results obtained via interviews (mentioned in the last paragraph) or the results obtained with the standardized questionnaires? Explain.

8. In light of the methodology, how much credence do you give to the finding that "the majority of survivors reported a mild level of posttraumatic stress syndrome"?

9. Does this study show that childhood cancer is a *cause* of stress? Explain.

Case 42

Studying the Sale of Alcoholic Beverages
to Minors[1]

Problem: Researchers wanted to study the sale of alcohol to underage minors. They decided to have supervised underage minors attempt to purchase alcohol at retail establishments. This created several problems that are described below.

The Research Method: "During a l-week period ... 46 liquor stores and package goods stores were visited by one of two 19-year-old males who attempted to purchase a six-pack of beer. These young men were volunteer students working as interns in the County Prosecutor's Office. They did not appear old for their age, did not use false identification, and did not attempt to deceive the salesperson in any other way, such as growing facial hair or altering their appearance to look older.

"If salespeople requested identification, the young men stated that they were not carrying any and left the premises. Each person was wearing a recording device so that his exchange with the salesperson was recorded. If a purchase was made, the young man gave the alcoholic beverage to an investigator from the County Prosecutor's Office who was driving the young man's car. Both minors were given breathalyzer tests at the beginning and end of each day of the operation. All the tests were negative.

"The 46 outlets visited (representing approximately 20-30% of all licensed establishments) were selected from 16 of the 24 municipalities in the county. Within each municipality, the selection of establishments was random. The range of outlets selected in each of the 16 municipalities ranged from one to six (with a mode of two). The establishments received no prior warning of the operation. Attempts to purchase were made during both the afternoon and the evening.

"The minors were successful in purchasing alcohol in 27 (58.7%) of the 46 establishments visited. The group of 27 consisted of 6 liquor stores, 3 convenience stores, 2 franchise operations, and 16 bars. Twenty-three of the stores where a purchase was made were visited again the next day. This time, 18 (78.3%) of the attempts were successful.

"Although limited to just one county in one state, and to a relatively small sample of retail establishments, the findings from this study concerning the sale of alcohol to minors are striking. They confirm accounts obtained from surveys that show that adolescents who wish to purchase alcohol can do so with relative ease.

---

[1] Source/reference: O'Leary, D., Gorman, D. M., & Speer, P. W. (1994). The sale of alcoholic beverages to minors. *Public Health Reports, 109*, 816–818.

"To our knowledge, this is only one of three research reports presenting a detailed account of the extent of sales of alcohol to those younger than the legal drinking age based on actual purchases from retail outlets. Our finding that almost 6 of 10 establishments were willing to sell alcohol to a minor gives clear cause for concern. Even more disturbing is the fact that another successful purchase was made at 78% of these locations the very next day. This suggests that certain stores may provide easier access to alcohol than others—something that is likely to be common knowledge among local underage drinkers…

"New Jersey law prohibits persons younger than age 21 years from purchasing and possessing alcoholic beverages, with violators subject to a fine of between $100 and $1,000 and a maximum jail term of 6 months.

"The 19-year-olds making the purchases in our study had to be granted immunity under state statutes and closely supervised by the County Prosecutor's Office. This supervision included the purchasers wearing a recording device to monitor the actual purchase attempt. Under New Jersey law, the use of such devices requires the consent of one of the parties to the conversation (in this case, the purchaser) and the approval of the County Prosecutor. As to granting immunity from prosecution, prosecuting attorneys in New Jersey, as in other states, have the authority when it is considered to be in the interest of justice. (The practice is most commonly employed when the state is prosecuting codefendants). In fact, employment of this procedure to limit the sale of alcoholic beverages to adolescents would appear to be fairly widespread in the United States, with a recent survey showing that officials from 24 of 51 alcohol enforcement agencies (50 states plus the District of Columbia) reported the use of undercover operations that involved purchase attempts by minors…

"Various precautions were taken during the course of our undercover operation to ensure that at no point did the underage person who entered the establishment consume any alcohol. We tape-recorded the exchange between the salesperson and the minor, and gave the minor a breathalyzer test. In addition, precautions were taken so as to avoid charges of entrapment on the part of the salesperson, such as choosing underage operatives who did not appear old for their age.

"In regard to that point, it is worth noting that at their initial court appearance, slightly more than half of the 46 people who had sold alcohol to the minors did indeed plead not guilty, claiming that they were entrapped because the underage operatives would have appeared older than age 21 to any reasonable person. At the subsequent court appearance, all the defendants pleaded guilty when confronted with the purchasers. Thus, once the minors were present, none of the defendants was willing to claim in court that they appeared older than age 21 years. In addition, it did not prove necessary to use the recording of the purchase attempt in any of the prosecutions."

Your Opinions:

1. The researchers state that the 46 outlets were selected at random from all outlets within 16 of the 24 municipalities in a county. If the researchers wished to generalize to all outlets in the county, would it be important to know whether the 16 municipalities were selected at random from the 24 municipalities in the county? Explain.

2. The attempts to purchase alcoholic beverages were made during the afternoons and evenings. In your opinion, could the exclusion of mornings have affected the results? Explain.

3. It was legal to use 19-year-olds in this study because of a grant of immunity. In your opinion, was it ethical? Explain.

4. As a consumer of this research, would you be interested in knowing some of the demographics of the two 19-year-olds such as race and ethnicity? Explain.

5. As a consumer of this research, would you be interested in knowing how mature acting the 19-year-olds were? Is it possible that a mature, self-confident 19-year-old might be more successful in making a purchase than an immature one? Does this issue matter given that it is illegal to sell to a 19-year-old regardless of his or her maturity?

6. An alternative approach to this research topic is to use cohorts who were 21 years or over but *looked like* they were under 21. Are there advantages and disadvantages to this alternative? Explain.

7. What is your opinion on the ethics of having the 19-year-olds wear recording devices?

8. In research on some illegal activities (such as illicit drug use), it is uncommon for researchers to provide information they collect to law enforcement officials for possible prosecution. Speculate on why it was done in this case.

9. The researchers "followed-up" on those who sold alcohol to minors by referring them to the criminal justice system. Would a follow-up of those who did *not* sell alcohol to the minors (such as their demographics, their experiences with this issue, and so on) also be of interest to you as a consumer of this research? Explain.

10. If you were conducting this research, is there anything you would have done differently in addition to any things you may have already mentioned in your answers to earlier questions?

Case 43

Identifying Heroin Addicts Who
Falsify Information[1]

Problem: Researchers wanted to evaluate a treatment program sponsored by the National Institute on Drug Abuse that provided free methadone maintenance to individuals who inject heroin. "Subjects were recruited through outreach to local service providers (e.g., AIDS service organizations, social welfare programs, health clinics), flier distribution, and client word-of-mouth." By law and for the purposes of the study, only those who belonged to one or more of four groups were eligible: "individuals who were HIV-positive, gay or bisexual males, sex workers (prostitutes), or sex partners of individuals in the above three groups." A problem was that many who did not belong to four designated groups might lie in order to gain access to the free methadone maintenance program. Methadone is a synthetic drug that is used as a substitute for heroin in drug treatment programs; although it is addictive, it is less addictive than heroin. Moving heroin addicts off heroin and onto methadone helps them "step-down" to a drug that is easier to wean them from in drug treatment programs.

A Solution: "Prospective subjects were asked to complete an eligibility screening, in which a research interviewer evaluated their eligibility for methadone maintenance treatment...

"Subjects who claimed to be HIV-positive were asked to produce medical documentation. We used several techniques to verify claims that individuals engaged in sex work or had high-risk sex partners. For example, individuals claiming to engage in sex work were asked what they typically charged and how many customers ('dates') they would have over the course of an average week. Individuals who provided answers that were excessive on either count were questioned further to provide more detailed information. In many cases, obvious liars were rejected for project admission (e.g., when providing exorbitant amounts of money earned for sex work). We also attempted to disguise the actual reason for rejection in order to limit the spread of information on criteria for admission. For example, when an applicant was rejected for admission, we would say that our research design required individuals of particular age, gender, or race categories, which were determined by a selection process beyond the intake worker's control.

---

[1] Source/reference: Grella, C. E., Chaiken, S., & Anglin, M. D. (1995). A procedure for assessing the validity of self-report data on high-risk sex behaviors from heroin addicts entering free methadone treatment. *Journal of Drug Issues*, *25*, 723–733. Reprinted by permission.

"Individuals who were only eligible by virtue of their claim to have a high-risk sex partner were often asked to bring their partner in for an additional eligibility screening in order to substantiate their claim.

"Eligible subjects were informed that they would receive free methadone throughout the duration of the study and were asked to provide informed consent to participate in the research study. Research participation consisted of an intake interview approximately one month after admission and one or two follow-up interviews, dependent upon when they entered the project. The follow-up interviews were conducted approximately 18 and 36 months after treatment admission.

"At the intake interview, all subjects were urged to provide honest and accurate information, and assured that, even if they admitted to providing false information at the eligibility screening, their status in the project would not be jeopardized. That is, no subjects were involuntarily discharged from treatment because they admitted to lying in order to gain admission to the project. We discussed with them the need for accurate data in order to conduct a meaningful evaluation of the treatment project. By stressing the importance of good treatment evaluation for helping others like themselves, we used a variant of Nurco's (1988) 'appealing to altruism' approach to increase the validity of drug users' self-reports. This process continued throughout successive follow-up interviews, at which subjects were again urged to provide accurate information and reassured that no penalties would occur if they admitted to earlier falsification.

"It became apparent to us that many applicants to the program were aware that reporting high-risk behaviors was the key to obtaining treatment admission. Prospective subjects were, therefore, highly motivated to misrepresent their risk status to gain entrance to a free methadone maintenance treatment program. In order to measure the prevalence of subjects' falsification of self-reported high-risk sex behaviors at the eligibility screening, we instituted a procedure to cross-check this information with data collected in subsequent interviews. Information obtained at the intake and follow-up interviews regarding high-risk sex behaviors (e.g., engaging in male homosexual behavior, exchanging sex for money or drugs) was compared with information provided at the eligibility screening.

"During interviews, individuals who spontaneously admitted to lying were coded as 'falsifiers' and their target group membership reassessed. Further, they were asked to provide accurate information on any variable that had been previously falsified (e.g., number of sex partners; whether they had engaged in male homosexual activity; amount of income from illegal activity, such as prostitution; and whether they had a sex partner of high risk). Individuals who provided information inconsistent with their initial eligibility screening were confronted with this inconsistency and asked which self-assessment accurately reflected their behavior. An individual who continued to provide highly inconsistent information or who appeared to be evasive was coded as a 'suspected falsifier.'

"Overall, 160 (32%) of the total sample of 500 were classified as 'falsifiers' because they either spontaneously admitted to lying, admitted to lying after being confronted, or were strongly suspected of lying in their eligibility screening. Of these, 106 or 66% did not meet criteria for membership in any of the four priority target groups; the other 54 were actually eligible for admission based on behavior that qualified them for membership in at least one other target group. The rate of admitted and/or suspected falsifiers for each of the four target groups is as follows: 4 (1%) falsely claimed to be HIV-positive; 66 (13%) falsely claimed they were gay or bisexual males; 111 (22%) falsely claimed to be sex workers; and 40 (8%) falsely claimed to be a sex partner of a high-risk individual."

Falsifiers were compared with nonfalsifiers on a number of variables. "Falsifiers were significantly more likely to be male and older, compared with others admitted into the project. No racial differences were found. Falsifiers reported less...income... Falsifiers did not differ in their criminal behavior, treatment motivation, needle use, frequency of condom use, or on" any of the personality variables that were measured in the study.

Your Opinions:

1. Before reading this case, would you have anticipated that a large percentage of prospective subjects might lie to gain admission to the program? Explain.

2. Are there other types of programs (other than those for illicit drug users) for which prospective subjects might lie in order to gain admission? Explain.

3. Assuming that all subjects were heroin addicts at intake, is it important that some who were selected as subjects had lied to gain admission to the program? Do these individuals introduce error into the study on the effectiveness of the program? Explain.

4. Is the requirement to provide medical documentation a foolproof way to determine whether subjects are indeed HIV-positive? Are there other ways to determine this? Explain.

5. In your opinion, is there a danger in excluding those who gave excessive accounts of the number of "dates" they have during a week and the amounts that they are paid? Explain.

6. Those who claimed to have a high-risk sexual partner were often asked to bring their partner in for screening. Are there advantages and disadvantages to doing this? Explain.

7. In your opinion, does the fact that the researchers lied about the reasons for rejection (i.e., falsely stating that applicants were rejected because of the requirements of the research design) pose any ethical problems? Explain.

8. What is your opinion on the use of "appealing to altruism" to increase the validity of self-reports for this population? Is it better than using threats such as possible expulsion from the program? Explain.

9. Despite the researchers' efforts during the eligibility screening, 32% of the sample was subsequently classified as "falsifiers." Does this surprise you? Explain.

10. Are there any other methods the researchers could have used to identify more "falsifiers" during the preliminary eligibility screening?

11. In your opinion, how likely is it that some of the 68% who were *not* classified as falsifiers were, in reality, falsifiers?

Case 44

Observing Children's Aggressiveness
on the Playground[1]

Problem: Researchers wanted to study children's aggressiveness during unstructured free play on school playgrounds. They noted that while children's aggressiveness has been studied in laboratories, where the play activities are often contrived, "children's playground behaviors are markedly understudied even though they have important implications for development." One reason that it is understudied is the difficulty of following children moving freely across the relatively large areas of school playgrounds; even if they can be seen across the playgrounds, it is difficult, if not impossible, to hear what they say.

A Solution: "We conducted observations at two [elementary] schools with playgrounds that measured approximately 70 x 100 m. The camera was set up in classrooms overlooking the playground. Two observers were required at all times: One researcher operated the camera, and the other researcher remained on the playground to place the microphones on the target children and assist in tracking them. The researcher on the playground carried a list of names of children to be observed. On locating a target child, the researcher approached the child and asked whether he or she would be willing to wear the microphone for a period of 10 minutes. The researcher then switched on the transmitter, placed it on the child, and clipped the microphone to the child's clothing. Children were instructed to play as they normally would. All children knew they were being filmed. In the course of conversation with the child, the researcher mentioned the child's name and identified the color of the child's clothes. This identifying information was essential to track target children among the approximately 250 children on the playground.

"We encountered several ethical concerns in developing the remote observational methodology: obtaining consent, duty to report, and limits of communication. The advantage of remote naturalistic observations is that children's behaviors are not constrained. At the same time, children other than those targeted for the research may enter the camera frame. Their presence poses a problem with respect to obtaining informed consent. One solution is to obtain consent for all the children in the school. If some parents do not consent to their child's participation, the researcher is obliged to avoid gathering data on these children. It may be possible to discard film segments with children for whom there

[1] Source/reference: Pepler, D., & Craig, W. M. (1995). A peek behind the fence: Naturalistic observations of aggressive children with remote audiovisual recording. *Developmental Psychology*, *31*, 548–553. Copyright © 1995 by the American Psychological Association, Inc. Reprinted with permission.

is no consent or to prevent these children from going onto the playground during filming. The former strategy requires the costly and difficult task of identifying all children. The latter strategy places artificial constraints on children's interactions: Friends of the target may not be present on the playground. Under these circumstances, the disadvantages are similar to those for contrived play-group situations in which the external validity of the observations is jeopardized. Because the research projects in which we have used this methodology have all been integral to intervention and prevention programs being offered within the school, we have been able to obtain *in loco parentis* consent from the school principal for those children not directly involved in the observational research. Within pure research studies, however, the task of obtaining consent for all children may be too formidable to make this methodology viable.

"Teachers and supervising adults must also be informed about the nature of the research. If some of these adults do not consent, the aforementioned strategies may be used. For example, teachers who do not consent might be removed from yard duty during filming.

"A second ethical issue concerns duty to warn… In conducting observations of aggressive children's playground interactions, one may observe interactions in which children's safety is a concern (e.g., extreme aggression or weapons). [Previous researchers have] acknowledged a similar concern within a laboratory situation. Researchers, in conjunction with the school staff, can develop definitions of situations that merit duty to warn and procedures to be followed. These procedures should address the ethical responsibility of duty to warn, while at the same time maintaining the integrity of the research. We developed procedures to inform the supervising adults on the playground concerning harmful and dangerous behaviors. This strategy protected the children, while at the same time alleviating direct involvement by the researchers.

"A final ethical concern is clarifying the limits of communication… To ensure confidentiality for the children and teachers filmed, we did not show our tapes to the school staff, children, or parents involved in the study. Hence, the schools were not able to use the tapes as a form of surveillance to assess, diagnose, or determine treatment plans for individual children. The consent form specified that the tapes would be used for research and educational purposes only.

"Remote audiovisual observations provide a unique opportunity to observe children's interactions that generally occur beyond our view. The primary strength of this observational methodology is its external validity. Children being observed are completely mobile on the school playground and are able to choose the activities and partners for their play. Aggression is thought to occur relatively infrequently on school playgrounds… With the ability to 'peek' into the playground, we were able to observe the full range of aggressive behaviors and to determine that aggression is not a rare event… The efficacy of this methodology was apparent in our study of bullying on the playground. Although significantly fewer girls than boys admit to bullying on surveys,…we observed girls bullying at the same rate as boys… Studies of girls' aggressive behaviors are notably scant, perhaps because we lack the appropriate tools for detecting and understanding girls' aggression. This methodology, which captures the subtle forms of verbal and indirect aggression, may prove particularly effective in our attempts to understand the complexities of girls' aggression."

Your Opinions:

1. In their complete article (portions of which are shown above), the researchers state that their technique permits "naturalistic observations" as opposed to laboratory observations, in which "the experimenter has control over the children involved, the materials, the space for play, and the duration of the play period. Interactions can be easily heard and seen…" In your opinion, are there advantages and disadvantages to making naturalistic observations? Are there advantages and disadvantages to making laboratory observations? Explain.

2. In the above excerpt, the researchers indicate that their method has high "external validity." In their full article, they also state that laboratory observations have the advantage of having high "internal validity." If you have a research methods book, look up *external validity* and *internal validity*. In your opinion, are the researchers correct in their assessment of the external and internal validity of the two methods for making observations? Explain.

3. In your opinion, does having children wear microphones limit the "naturalness" of the observations? If yes, are the microphones likely to seriously reduce the validity of the resulting data? Explain.

4. Is having children wear a microphone likely to yield better data than having an adult observer on the playground try to stay close enough to the children to overhear the children's conversations? Explain.

5. In the second paragraph, the researchers note that they were able to obtain *in loco parentis* consent from the principal for those children not directly involved in the observational research. Do you think this is an adequate type of consent for the researchers' purpose? Explain.

6. Have the researchers addressed to your satisfaction all potential ethical problems raised by their methodology? Explain.

7. The researchers note that "fewer girls than boys admit to bullying on [previous] surveys." However, with naturalistic observations, they found that girls were bullying as much as boys. Does this convince you that the survey data are incorrect? Do these findings convince you that naturalistic observation is superior to using surveys for studying children's aggressiveness? Explain.

8. Are there any reasons why a researcher might prefer to use surveys rather than observational methods to gather data on aggressiveness? Explain.

9. Speculate on why "studies of girls' aggressive behavior are notably scant." Do you agree that this might be the result of the lack of appropriate tools for studying this behavior? Explain.

Introducing Participants to a Study on Lie Telling[1]

Problem: Researchers wanted to study the relationship between lie telling in everyday life and other personality variables. Since lying is generally regarded as socially undesirable, the researchers needed to introduce the study in such a way that participants would be open to disclosing their lie-telling behavior.

Introduction to the Study: "The Study 1 participants and the participants from Study 2 who were recruited from the community college initially responded to notices describing the research that were posted on a bulletin board in an academic building. The study was described as one in which they would keep records of their social interactions and communications for 7 days. In Study 1, the notice indicated that participants would receive partial course credit for their participation, and, in Study 2, the notice indicated that participants would be paid $35. Study 2 participants recruited from continuing education lists or from the phone directory were sent letters with the same description of the research, and then they were contacted by telephone about a week later.

"All participants attended an initial 90-minute meeting, conducted by one or more members of the research team, in which the study and the procedures were explained. In Study 1, these were group sessions attended by 10-15 participants at a time. The Study 2 sessions were conducted individually or in small groups. When participants arrived for this session, they spent the first 20 minutes answering the personality and demographic questionnaires. The study was then explained in full. Anyone who needed more time to complete the individual-differences measures did so at the end of the session.

"Participants were told that they would be recording all of their social interactions and all of the lies that they told during those interactions every day for a week. It was noted that their role in this research was especially important in that they would be the observers and recorders of their own behavior. The investigators explained that they did not condone or condemn lying; rather, they were studying it scientifically and trying to learn the answers to some of the most fundamental questions about the phenomenon. They encouraged the participants to think of the study as an unusual opportunity to learn more about themselves.

"The key terms were then explained to the participants. A social interaction was defined as 'any exchange between you and another person that lasts 10 minutes or more ... in which the behavior of one person is in response to the behavior of another person.' This definition, plus many of the examples used to

---

[1] Source/reference: Kashy, D. A., & DePaulo, B. M. (1996). Who lies? *Journal of Personality and Social Psychology, 70,* 1037–1051 Copyright © 1996 by the American Psychological Association Inc. Reprinted by permission.

clarify the definition, was taken or adapted from that used in the initial studies involving the Rochester Interaction Record... We did add an exception to the 10-minute rule: For any interaction in which participants told a lie, they were to fill out a social interaction record, even if the interaction lasted less than 10 minutes. Copies of our adaptation of the RIR...were then distributed, and participants were told how to fill out the form.

"To explain what participants should count as a lie, it was noted that 'a lie occurs any time you intentionally try to mislead someone. Both the intent to deceive and the actual deception must occur.' More than a dozen examples of lies were given, including examples of kind and unkind lies and lies motivated by many different types of concerns. Participants were urged to record all lies, no matter how big or how small. They were instructed that if they were uncertain as to whether a particular communication qualified as a lie, they should record it. (At the end of the study, two of the investigators independently read through all of the lie diaries and agreed on the few that did not meet the definition and were therefore excluded.) The definition that we gave participants was interpreted broadly as encompassing any intentional attempts to mislead, including even nonverbal ones. The only example of a lie they were asked not to record was saying 'fine' in response to perfunctory 'How are you?' questions. Participants completed one deception record for every lie that they told. Sample [forms]...were distributed, and the investigators explained how to fill them out.

"Participants were instructed to fill out the forms (social interaction records and deception records) at least once a day; it was suggested that they set aside a particular time or set of times to do so. The forms were then collected by the experimenters at several different times throughout the week. Participants were also given pocket-sized notebooks and urged to carry them at all times. They were encouraged to use these notebooks to write down reminders of their social interactions and their lies as soon as possible after the events had taken place. Then they could use their notes as an aid to their memory if they did not complete their social interaction and deception records until later in the day. The notebooks were not collected.

"Several additional steps were taken to encourage the reporting of all lies. First, participants were told that if they did not wish to reveal the contents of any of the lies that they told, then in the space on the deception record in which they were to describe their lie, they could instead write 'rather not say.' That way, we as investigators would still know that a lie was told, and we would know other information about the lie and the social interaction in which it was told (from the other parts of the records that the participants completed). Participants declined to describe only 1% of their lies in the college sample and none of their lies in the community sample. Second, we instructed participants that if they did not completely remember everything about a lie that they told, they should still fill out as much of the information on the form as they could. Third, we told participants that if they remembered a lie from a previous day that they had not recorded, they should still turn in a form for that lie.

"The importance of accuracy and conscientiousness in keeping the records was emphasized throughout the session. As a means of ensuring anonymity, participants chose their own identification number to be used throughout the study. Participants did not write their names on any of the forms.

"At the end of the session, the investigators reviewed the amount of time it would take to complete all phases of the study and encouraged participants to terminate their participation at that point if they no longer had the interest or the time to participate fully. They were offered credit or payment even if they chose not to continue. All participants elected to continue.

"Before they left, participants were given typed copies of all of the instructions and definitions they had been given during the session. This instruction booklet also included names and phone numbers of members of the research team with whom they had met and whom they could contact at any time with any questions or concerns they might have. Appointments were also made with all of the Study 1 participants to return once more at the end of the 7-day recording period to complete a final set of measures. Study 2 participants were shown an envelope and instructions that would be mailed to them at the end of the study so that they could complete the same measures."

Your Opinions:

1. The first sentence in the fifth paragraph contains the definition of a "lie" given to the participants. What is your opinion of the definition?

2. The researcher states that "two of the investigators *independently* read through all of the lie diaries." In this context, what does *independently* mean? Is it important to read independently? Explain.

3. Speculate on why participants were instructed to fill out the forms "at least once a day." Is this better than having them fill out forms at the end of each interaction in which a lie is told? Is it better than having them fill out forms only at the end of the weeklong study? Explain.

4. Was it a good idea to allow participants to record "rather not say"? Were you surprised that such a small percentage recorded this? Explain.

5. Was it a good idea to offer credit or payment even if participants chose not to participate after the study was introduced? Explain.

6. Are there advantages and disadvantages to using diaries as a means of collecting data on lie-telling behavior? Explain.

7. Are there methods for collecting data on lie-telling behavior other than using diaries? Are these methods superior to using diaries? Explain.

8. Overall, do you think the researchers conducted the study in such a way that the participants would generally be truthful about their lie-telling behavior? Explain.

9. To what population or populations should the results of this study be generalized? Explain.

Case 46

Measuring Sex-Role Stereotyping
Among Children[1]

Background: Numerous researchers have studied children's sex-role stereotypes using self-report measures. The following excerpt from a journal article critiques some methods used to study this variable.

Research Methods: "Among those measures aimed at assessing sex typing of others, one important issue concerns the differences in the way in which questions are phrased and the response options available to respondents. Questions used to elicit children's sex typing of others have included questions such as 'Who should be a…?,' 'Who can be a…?,'and 'Who likes to…?'

"In earlier work with my colleagues…, we argued that existing measures of children's sex typing of others did not all tap the same construct. Instead, we believed that…measures could be classified into two groups: (a) those that assess children's *knowledge* of societal gender stereotypes and (b) those that assess children's *personal attitudes* toward gender roles. Specifically, we argued that *knowledge* of societal stereotypes is assessed when children are (a) asked 'Who usually…?' performs various occupations or activities, or possesses various traits, *and/or* (b) forced to respond by choosing one or the other sex. We argued that gender-role *attitudes* are assessed when children are asked 'Who can…?' or 'Who should…?' perform various occupations or activities, or possess various traits *and* are given the option of assigning items to both sexes.

"Findings [of earlier studies] indicated that the two types of methodologies were associated with distinct patterns of responding. When children were forced to choose one sex or the other (i.e., there was no 'both men and women' option), stereotyped responding increased with age. On the other hand, when children were given the response option of 'both men and women,' the opposite pattern emerged—stereotyped responding decreased with age, especially when the question form was 'Who should…?' or 'Who can…?'

"Another crucial issue in developmental research on gender is the comprehensibility of the measures given to children and younger adolescents… It seems likely that several…measures have problems with regard to children's interpretation of the questions posed. One concern is that the items included on the scales are developmentally appropriate. The domain of occupations stereotyping often includes items such as 'nurse,' 'secretary,' and even 'stockbroker'… Some

---

[1] Source/reference: Bigler, R. S. (1997). Conceptual and methodological issues in the measurement of children's sex typing. *Psychology of Women Quarterly*, *21*, 53–69. Copyright © 1997 by Division 35, American Psychological Association, Inc. Reprinted with the permission of Cambridge University Press.

research suggests that children's understanding of many sex-typed occupational labels is not consistent with that of adults or with the interpretation required by sex-typing measures... For example, a recent study...found that a number of elementary school children had little understanding of the term 'secretary,' and that some children believed the term 'nurse' to be the appropriate label for a female physician. Obviously, children's misunderstanding of scale items is likely to decrease the accuracy of sex-typing measures, particularly those measures that include few items.

"Finally, it seems important to repeat a caution made by this author and others about the possible negative effects of sex-typing measures... A recent study...found that the functional use of gender in the environment (i.e., pointing out and using gender in a gender-neutral context) increases children's gender stereotyping... Most researchers working in this area probably have a commitment to avoid exacerbating the problem of gender stereotyping, and thus it is important to consider ways to ameliorate the potential negative effects on children or adults participating in research of this kind. ...investigators might routinely use debriefing sessions—even with children—in which there is a more extensive discussion of the issues underlying the work. For example, the reasons for requesting responses by gender could be explained, and alternative categorizations (or even reasons why gender might be irrelevant) discussed."

Your Opinions:

1. In your opinion, how important is the distinction between "Who usually performs...?" and "Who can perform...?" Explain.

2. In your opinion, might some young children respond to "Who can perform...?" on the basis of their *knowledge* of who usually performs an occupation? In other words, might some children be insensitive to the distinction between *who can perform* and *who usually performs*? Explain.

3. The writer suggests that "Who should...?" and "Who can...?" are both acceptable for measuring *personal attitudes* toward gender stereotypes. In your opinion are they both equally good? Explain.

4. In addition to including the choices "Men," "Women," and "Both men and women," would it be a good idea to also include this choice: "Don't know"? Explain.

5. In your opinion, would it help to provide definitions of terms such as "nurse," and "stockbroker" in measures of sex typing? If yes, would it be acceptable to define a "nurse" as "someone who helps a doctor" in a measure for use with young children? If you agree that providing definitions is a good idea, how would you define "stockbroker"?

6. The researchers note that the problem of comprehensibility is especially important when measures contain only a few items. In addition to "nurse," "secretary," and "stockbroker," what other occupations might be included in a measure for children?

7. The writer states that the comprehensibility of the questions is a crucial issue in *developmental research*. In such research, researchers look for differences across age groups or across developmental stages. Is the validity of developmental research threatened if children's understandings of questions on sex-typing change as they grow older? Explain.

8. In addition to using self-report measures, are there other ways to get information on the sex-typing attitudes that children hold? Explain.

9. In your opinion, is the risk of exacerbating the problem of gender stereotyping in samples of participants in these types of studies justified by the need to know about gender stereotyping? (In other words, is it justifiable to risk harming relatively small samples of children in order to learn more about a problem that may affect large numbers of children?) Explain.

10. Do you believe that debriefing sessions would be helpful for ameliorating the potential negative effects on children in such studies? If yes, should the debriefing be conducted before or after the sex-typing attitudes are measured? Explain.

Notes:

Case 47

Studying Suicide Ideation and Acculturation Among Adolescents[1]

Background: Researchers explored the relationship between suicide ideation and acculturation among Mexican-American adolescents. In the introduction to their research report, they note that "Variables believed to be related to suicidal behavior that are prevalent more among Hispanic Americans and other minority groups than among non-Hispanic Whites include poverty, language difficulties that can contribute to feelings of estrangement, ethnic identity concerns, and discrimination... Furthermore, correlates of poverty such as depression and substance use/abuse theoretically might influence some Hispanic adolescents to experience even more emotional distress, thereby increasing their risk for suicidal thoughts or suicide attempts. In addition to those stressors, some Hispanic adolescents may endure stress related to the pressures to acculturate and to conflicts with their relatively less acculturated parents... All things considered, Hispanic youth possibly may be a subgroup of adolescents who could be more susceptible to suicidal behavior than are adolescents in general..."

Research Methods: "Prior to conducting this study, formal approval was granted by the institutional review board of the researchers' university and by the superintendent of the school district where this study took place. The principal researcher introduced the study to students during the life skills segment of their regular curriculum. Lessons in this segment typically include topics such as substance abuse and self-esteem. The students were told that they could volunteer to take part in a study on suicide ideation and acculturation. One week later, during the life skills period, three teachers administered the questionnaires in their classes to the students who had returned signed parental consent forms. A total of 28 [eighth graders] out of 270 did not participate; the nonparticipants worked separately on other class assignments during the study.

"Participants were informed that the information they provided on the questionnaires would be confidential, and they were instructed not to provide any identifying information on the questionnaires so as to maintain their anonymity. The participants were also informed that if they found themselves feeling sad or being concerned about thoughts that bothered them either during or after the study, they were encouraged to visit the school counselor to discuss their feelings or concerns. Each item on all the questionnaires was read aloud to the participants by

---

[1] Source/reference: Rasmussen, K. M., Negy, C., Carlson, R., & Burns, J. M. (1997). Suicide ideation and acculturation among low socioeconomic status Mexican-American adolescents. *Journal of Early Adolescence, 17,* 390–407. Copyright © 1997 by Sage Publications, Inc. Excerpt reprinted with permission of Sage Publications, Inc.

their respective teachers to accommodate participants with possible reading difficulties. (Students tracked in an English as a Second Language curriculum do not attend the classes that participated in this study; therefore, only students who were functionally fluent in English participated.) The participants' respective teachers publicly responded to any relevant questions the participants had. It took approximately 45 minutes to complete the questionnaires."

A suicidal ideation questionnaire contained 15 statements such as "I wished I were dead," "I thought that killing myself would solve my problems," and "I thought it would be better if I were not alive." Students responded to each statement on a scale from 0 = *I never had this thought* to 6 = *Almost every day*. Students were also administered an acculturation questionnaire, which contained these questions: (a) "What language do you speak?"; (b) "In what language do you think?"; (c) "How do you identify yourself?"; (d) "Which ethnic identification does (did) your mother use?"; and (e) "Which ethnic identification does (did) your father use?" In addition, questionnaires on depression and self-esteem were administered.

Your Opinions:

1. In your opinion, could some students be seriously harmed by their participation in this study? Explain.

2. If you answered yes to question 1, do you think that the researchers took adequate precautions to protect the participants from harm? Explain.

3. In your opinion, is any potential harm to the participants outweighed by the need for information on the relationship between acculturation and suicide ideation?

4. Because the questions were read aloud, the 28 who declined to participate may have heard the questions even though they were not responding to them. Is this problematic in terms of their right to refuse to be in the study? Explain.

5. When obtaining informed consent, researchers usually tell potential participants that they have the right to withdraw from the study at any time. Based on the information reported by the researchers, does it seem likely that students knew they could withdraw even while the questionnaires were being administered? Explain.

6. Suppose that while scoring the questionnaires on suicide ideation, the researchers found a student with an extremely high score. In your opinion, do the researchers have an obligation to try to identify the student so that he or she can be referred to a professional for help? Do they have a right to try to identify the student? Explain.

7. The researchers point out that they only studied students who were functionally fluent in English. Speculate on why they did this. Could this decision affect the outcome of the study? Explain.

8. What is your opinion on the measure of acculturation used in this study?

9. The researchers state that the teachers publicly responded to any questions the students had. Does allowing teachers to answer questions during the administration of the questionnaires pose any problems? Does it have any advantages? Explain.

Notes:

Case 48

Encouraging Truthfulness in Telephone Interviews[1]

Problem: Researchers assumed "that adults underreport most, but not all, aspects of their sexual behavior. This assumption is based on the perspective that people in our culture view sexual activity as a private behavior or as a somewhat 'questionable' behavior that one either should not be doing or should not be doing too much of. Evidence indicates that adults typically underreport their sexual activities, including both positive and negative sexual events…"

The researchers noted that "in national probability surveys, adult men, relative to women, tend to report greater numbers of sexual partners…and, among people with risk factors for HIV/STDs, men are more likely to report using condoms (i.e., women report more nonuse than men)… Thus, men may be overreporting their numbers of sexual partners and their condom use (or women may be underreporting)."

Research Methods: The researchers "obtained 2,030 English-speaking respondents 18–49 years old from a random-digit [telephone] dialing sample of the contiguous United States…"

Because the gender of the interviewer might affect the honesty of respondents' answers, some respondents were randomly assigned to have a same-gender interviewer, some were randomly assigned to have an opposite-gender interviewer, and the remaining ones were given a choice of whether they wanted to be interviewed by a male or female interviewer. The latter group was told, "Because some of the questions we will be asking are somewhat personal, we want you to choose the kind of interviewer you would like. We have found that some people prefer male interviewers and others prefer female interviewers. Would you like to have a female interviewer or a male interviewer?

"Respondents were also randomly assigned to either enhanced-item-wording ($N = 1,000$) or standard-item-wording ($N = 1,030$). The standard survey was based on items from well-known AIDS and human sexuality studies…" The enhanced items were designed to convey "a less judgmental and more positive spin" in order to encourage honest answers. Samples of standard and enhanced items are shown in Table 1.

[1] Source/reference: Catania, J. A., Binson, D., Canchola, J., Pollack, L. M., Hauck, W., & Coates, T. J. (1996). Effects of interviewer gender, interviewer choice, and item wording on responses to qustions concerning sexual behavior. *Public Opinion Quarterly*, *60*, 345–375. Copyright © 1996 American Association of Public Opinion Research. Published by University of Chicago Press.

Table 1   Examples of Standard and Enhanced Questions Used in the Survey

Enhanced Questions	Standard Questions
[Ask if heterosexual male.] In past surveys, many men have reported that at some point in their life they have had some type of sexual experience with another male. This could have happened before adolescence, during adolescence, or as an adult. Have you ever had sex of any kind with a male at some point in your life?	[Ask if heterosexual male.] Have you ever had sex of any kind with another male?
Many people feel that being sexually faithful to a spouse is important and some do not. However, even those who think being faithful is important have found themselves in situations where they ended up having sex with someone other than their (husband/wife). At any time while you were married during the past 10 years, did you have sex with someone other than your (husband/wife)?	At any time while you were married during the past 10 years, did you have sex with someone other than your (husband/wife)?

Your Opinions:

1. In addition to sexual behavior, are there other types of behavior that might be as prone to over- or underreporting? Explain.

2. In general, do you think that the gender of the interviewer is an important variable in a study of this type?

3. What is your opinion on the *first* enhanced question? Do you think that the researchers achieved their objective of writing an item that conveys "a less judgmental and more positive spin" than the standard item? Do you think that the enhanced item is a "leading" question? (Note: Authors of research methods books warn against using leading questions, that is, questions that point the respondent in one direction or another.) If you think it is leading, do you think it is justifiable in this case since men may underreport sex with other men when asked the question in a standard format?

4. Considering your answer to question 3, would you have more faith overall in the honesty of the answers to the standard question or to the enhanced question? Explain.

5. What is your opinion on the *second* enhanced question in Table 1? Do you think that the researchers achieved their objective of writing an item that conveys "a less judgmental and more positive spin" than the standard item? Do you think that the enhanced item is a "leading" question? If you think it is leading, do you think it is justifiable to use such a leading question in this case since men and women may underreport infidelity to a spouse when asked the question in a standard format?

6. As it turns out, 6.2 % of the men who were asked the first enhanced question answered "yes," while only 3.3% of the men asked the standard form of the question answered "yes." (These results are for all men regardless of whether the interviewer was male or female.) In your opinion, does this indicate that the enhanced question was superior to the standard question in getting honest responses?

7. As it turns out, 5.9% of men who were asked the first question by a male interviewer answered "yes." (This percentage is for all men who had a male interviewer regardless of the question form.) The comparable percentage for men who had a female interviewer was 3.6%. In your opinion, does this indicate that using a male interviewer was superior in getting honest responses?

8. Suppose you were going to conduct a survey on this topic. To measure extramarital sexual activity, would you use the standard question, the enhanced question, or some other form of question that you would devise? Explain.

9. In addition to controlling gender of the interviewer and using care in the wording of questions, are there any other measures that might be taken to encourage honest answers to questions on sexual behavior? Explain.

Notes:

Case 49

Estimating the Credibility of Young Children's Reports[1]

Problem: The credibility of young children's reports is a crucial factor in some criminal cases, especially in cases of child sexual abuse, where the child may be the only witness of the actual events. Researchers have conducted studies to help gain an understanding of their credibility, including the extent to which children might be susceptible to the influence of an interviewer who asks leading questions. Note that in real cases, children may be engaging in denial or feel they need to keep information a secret. In such cases, using leading questions (such as "Where did she touch you?") instead of neutral questions (such as "Did she touch you?") might elicit more honest responses.

Approaches to the Research Problem: In early studies of the credibility of young children's reports, researchers questioned children about neutral events. For example, two researchers "found that preschoolers were progressively susceptible as the strength of misleading questions was increased. Thus, when four- to six-year-olds were asked about a nonexistent cabinet, only 6% falsely assented to the question, 'Is there a cabinet in the room?'; when asked, 'Isn't there a cabinet in the room?' the false assent rate rose to 25%. Finally, false answers reached a maximum of 56% when children were asked, 'Is the door open in the cabinet in the room?' A related point that is illustrated by the previous example is that the questioning of the children in the experimental settings seemed to bear little if any similarity to the conditions under which children are questioned in actual [criminal] cases.

"A recurring theme of these newer studies is the attempt to question children about the main actions that occurred during the experienced event rather than only about the peripheral details, such as the color of an actor's shoes. The ultimate challenge has been to ask questions in an ethically permissible manner about whether or not sexual actions occurred during these events.

"With great ingenuity, a number of researchers have met this challenge. For example, [researchers] questioned five- to seven-year-old girls about the details of a medical examination that for some children included a genital examination. The children were asked open-ended, direct, and misleading questions about touching and were also asked to demonstrate what happened to them by using anatomically detailed dolls. In [another] series of studies, [researchers] asked three- to

---

[1] Source/reference: Bruck, M., Ceci, S. J., & Hembrooke, H. (1998). Reliability and credibility of young children's reports: From research to policy and practice. *American Psychologist, 53*, 136–151. Copyright © 1998 by the American Psychological Association, Inc. Reprinted by permission.

seven-year-old children about their annual pediatric visits. These studies assessed the rate at which memories fade over different periods of delay as well as the degree to which children falsely include nonoccurring events as part of their reports.

"Thus, results of [these] studies provide data as to how accurately children report salient events, which may include bodily contact, when they are questioned immediately following the events or after up to a three-month delay. These data also reflect how accurately children respond to open-ended and both direct questions and misleading questions when they are questioned by a neutral, unbiased interviewer. Under these conditions, the children were fairly but not entirely accurate about a number of salient events that involved bodily touching. The results also show a typical pattern, found across many studies, in which children provide more information in response to specific compared with open-ended questions. For example, in [one] study, few children mentioned the genital examination in response to the question, 'Tell me everything that happened,' but many did provide the required information in response to more specific questions. However, although children generally provide more information to specific questions, it is generally the case that overall, accuracy rates are higher for responses to open-ended questions. Furthermore, accuracy of responses to specific and misleading questions increases as a function of age (with preschoolers being the least accurate) and as a function of the delay between the interview and the actual event. Some data indicate that when accuracy drops off, it is not merely the case that children forget and therefore make errors of omission (i.e., failing to recall an actual event), but they also make errors of commission (falsely claiming to have experienced a nonevent). In [one] study, children, especially the younger children, reported events that never happened. These reported nonevents included not only acts that could conceivably occur in a doctor's office but also acts that would not occur in the doctor's office and that would have connotations of abuse, at least to some adults (e.g., 'Did the doctor lick your knee?' 'Did the nurse sit on top of you?')."

Your Opinions:

1. Authors of research methods textbooks recommend against using leading questions when gathering data since the participants' responses may be affected by them. (The major exception would be when studying the effects of leading questions on the quality of the data obtained.) Despite this, do you think that the use of leading questions with young children in sexual abuse cases is justified? Explain.

2. The writer refers to the "ingenuity" of later researchers. Do you agree that their research is ingenious? Explain.

3. In one study, five- to seven-year-old girls were asked "misleading questions about touching." The purpose was to determine whether these children would continue to respond accurately in the face of an interviewer who was leading them. In your opinion, does this procedure pose an ethical problem? Explain.

4. In the later studies, children were questioned by a "neutral, unbiased interviewer," leading to the finding that children are "fairly" accurate about events involving bodily touching. In your opinion, is it safe to generalize this result to actual criminal cases where the interviewer may not be neutral? Explain.

5. Does it surprise you that young children provide more accurate answers to open-ended questions but provide more information to specific questions? In your opinion, does this have implications for interpreting children's reports in criminal cases?

6. In the studies, each child was questioned only once. In criminal investigations, a child may be questioned repeatedly by various people about alleged crimes. Does this limit the generalizability of the studies to the likely behavior of children involved in criminal investigations? Explain.

7. The latter studies involved medical settings. Are the results of these studies generalizable to nonmedical settings? Explain.

8. In general, do you think that the studies on this topic are important, given the necessary limitations in their methodology? Explain.

Notes:

Case 50

Designing an Experiment on Cross-Cultural Training[1]

Problem: Researchers wanted to determine the influence of cross-cultural training on the racial identity of White graduate students studying educational counseling. Their problem was to design a study that would allow them to determine whether the training was responsible for (i.e., *caused*) any differences they observed.

Approaches to the Research Problem:

"Participants were recruited from students pursuing a master's degree enrolled in two 16-week graduate-level multicultural counseling courses taught in a midsize Midwestern university. On the first day of class, the investigator (also the professor) informed students of the research project and requested their support. She emphasized that participation was voluntary, failure to participate would not influence course grades, and a pre- and posttest format would be used to collect data. A total of 41 White graduate counselors-in-training (28 women, 13 men) volunteered; but only 35 completed the pre- and posttests. The 35 participants who completed the pre- and posttests ranged in age from 22 to 47 years, with a mean age of 28.2 years. Of the 35, 34 indicated experience with one or more of the following ethnic or racial populations: (a) Black or African American ($n = 31$), (b) Hispanic or Latino American ($n = 28$), (c) Native American ($n = 11$), (d) Asian or Pacific Islander ($n = 22$). Of the group, 28 indicated that they had previous multicultural training in one or more of the following settings: (a) academia ($n = 18$), (b) agency ($n = 6$), (c) workshop ($n = 14$), (d) professional conference ($n = 10$).

"*White Racial Identity Attitude Scale* (WRIAS). The WRIAS measured White racial identity attitudes on five subscales: (a) **Contact**—obliviousness to racial-cultural issues, including the items, 'I hardly think about what race I am,' and 'I was raised to believe that people are people regardless of their race'; (b) **Disintegration**— awareness of the social implications of race on a personal level, with the items, 'I do not understand what Blacks want from Whites,' and 'Sometimes I am not sure what I think or feel about Black people'; (c) **Reintegration**—idealization of everything perceived to be White and denigration of everything thought to be Black, including the items, 'A Black person who tries to get close to you is usually after something,' and 'When I am the only White in a group of Blacks, I feel anxious'; (d) **Pseudoindependence**—internalization of

---

[1] Source/reference: Reprinted from Brown, S. P., Parham, T. A., & Yonker, R. (1996). Influence of a cross-cultural training course on racial identity attitudes of white women and men: Preliminary perspectives. *Journal of Counseling and Development, 74,* 510–516. Copyright © 1996 by the American Counseling Association.

Whiteness and capacity to recognize personal responsibility to ameliorate the consequences of racism with such items as, 'I enjoy watching the different ways that Blacks and Whites approach life,' and 'I feel comfortable talking to Blacks'; and (e) **Autonomy**—a bicultural or racially transcendent worldview, which includes the sample items, 'I involve myself in causes regardless of the race of the people involved in them,' and 'I am not embarrassed to admit that I am White.'

"The 50 items of the WRIAS assess attitudes on a 5-point Likert scale ranging from strongly disagree (1) to strongly agree (5)... Coefficient alpha reliabilities reported by Carter (1988) were .53, .77, .80, .71, and .67 for the Contact, Disintegration, Reintegration, Pseudoindependence, and Autonomy subscales. Although limited validity information exists for the WRIAS, the findings of Helms and Carter (1990) support content, construct, and criterion validity.

"*Assessment phase.* Participants were given 90 minutes during the first class meeting to complete the instruments. To obtain posttest data, participants were given 30 minutes during the last class meeting to complete the WRIAS.

"*Classroom intervention.* Recognizing the need to increase the cultural sensitivity of White counselors-in-training and the potential influence of these future practitioners on their racially diverse clients, a 16-week course was developed...

"Students met in a 3-hour class every week for 16 weeks. The instructional program was divided into three phases: self-awareness, knowledge of five ethnocultural populations (African American, Asian, Latino, Native American, and European American), and development of preliminary skills to counsel diverse clients. Phases 1 and 2 each lasted 5 weeks and Phase 3 lasted 6 weeks."

Analyzing the results for the five subscales separately for the men and women, the researchers found two significant differences: (1) women were significantly higher on the posttest than the pretest on *Pseudoindependence* (pretest mean = 3.50 and posttest mean = 3.77 on the scale from 1 to 5) and (2) men were significantly higher on the posttest than the pretest on *Autonomy* (pretest mean = 3.82 and posttest mean = 4.04). The other eight differences were not statistically significant.

"The results indicated that a cross-cultural counseling course changed, on the average, the racial identity attitudes of White counselors-in-training. Furthermore, the degree of impact seemed to be influenced by gender. Because racial identity attitude scores on the Autonomy and Pseudoindependence subscales of the WRIAS increased by the end of the semester, the female and male students in the study can be characterized as possessing enhanced abilities to (a) psychologically accept racial differences, (b) appreciate the potential impact of racial attitudes on people of color, and (c) exhibit less racist behaviors..."

Your Opinions:

1. One of the researchers was also the professor who was teaching the course in which the multicultural training was given. If you had been a student in such a course, would you have felt obligated to participate because you were being asked to do so by your professor? (Note that participation was voluntary and that the professor indicated that "failure to participate would not influence course grades." Also note that the WRIAS was administered during class meetings.)

2. Because the professor was evaluating the effects of a college course, would it have been ethical to require all students in the class to participate by completing the WRIAS? Explain.

3. Would you be interested in knowing why only 35 of the 41 volunteers completed both the pre- and posttests? Could the reason(s) affect your interpretation of the results? Explain.

4. Have the researchers given an adequate description of the reliability and validity of the WRIAS? Explain.

5. The researchers used a one-group pretest-posttest design. How could this design be improved?

6. How would you characterize the results? Would you say that they provide strong evidence that the training influenced the students' White racial identity? Explain.

7. Comment on the researchers' interpretation in the last paragraph. Is it supported by the data?

8. If you were conducting a follow-up study on the same topic, what changes in the research methodology would you make?

Notes:

Designing an Experiment on Worrying Among the Elderly[1]

Problem: A focus group interview is a measurement technique in which a small group of individuals participate in a semistructured interview. Unlike traditional interviews, the participants in a focus group interview are encouraged to share their ideas with each other in arriving at answers to the questions. Although it is a measurement technique, two researchers conducted a study using focus group participation as a *treatment* in a study. Specifically, their purpose was "to determine if elderly participants in a focus group discussion, designed to promote an in-depth exploration of worry and anxiety, reported long-term therapeutic benefits in their experience of worry." The researchers noted that "The only study to assess the effects of focus group participation found nonspecific short-term positive benefits… The long-term benefits of focus group discussions and their impact on the personal psychological lives of group members have not yet been assessed."

Method: The researchers studied a group of 21 "self-designated worriers (i.e., individuals who reported spending at least 5% of the day worrying) and who were over the age of seventy [with a mean age of 78.1].

"During the focus group discussion, participants were seated around a rectangular table with the discussion moderator (the second author). Two other experimenters sat unobtrusively off to the side, taking notes.

"The discussion began with a general question about what is difficult about being older these days. The following questions were introduced in the course of the discussion when each previous topic was exhausted: 1) What kinds of things do you worry about? 2) Is this worry common to people your age? 3) How can you tell when you are worried? 4) Can you differentiate between worry and anxiety and worry and depression? 5) Has the focus and frequency of your worry changed over your lifetime? 6) What kinds of things contribute to your worry? 7) What are the effects of worry on you? 8) What do you do to not worry and how do you stop it when it happens? 9) How would you define worry? The order of the presentation of these questions was dependent on the content of the discussion. The group discussions typically lasted an hour and a half."

"After the focus group interview, participants were debriefed, "names and addresses of participants who wanted a report of the results were retained.

---

[1] Source/reference: Powers, C. B., & Wisocki, P. A. (1997). An examination of the therapeutic benefits of focus groups on elderly worriers. *International Journal of Aging and Human Development, 45,* 159–167. Copyright © 1997, Baywood Publishing Co. Reprinted by permission.

Participants were thanked and given checks for $20.00 for their participation. Participants were also paid $5 for completing the pretest measures and $5 for the posttest measures."

The measures that were given as a pretest and a posttest were: (1) a single question that asked what percentage of a typical day they spend worrying; (2) a Worry Questionnaire that asked about worrying in the domains of health, finances, and social relationships; (3) a Life Satisfaction Questionnaire that asked about satisfaction in the areas of health, finances, social relationships, and religion; and (4) a symptom checklist with 90 items about psychological traits such as depression, anxiety, and paranoid ideation.

The posttest measures were taken 12 months after the focus group participation. About a third of those who participated in the focus group interview failed to return the posttest. The only statistically significant difference for those who took both the pretest and posttest was in the percent of the typical day spent worrying (with a mean of 21.0% on the pretest and a mean of 3.6% on the posttest, which was reported to be significant at the .01 level).

Your Opinions:

1. The study was confined to "self-designated worriers." Is this a flaw in the research methodology? Explain.

2. In the second and third paragraphs under the heading "Method," the researchers describe the focus group treatment. Is it adequately described? Do you believe that it is sufficiently operational (that is, described in terms of specific physical steps taken to give the treatment)?

3. The stated purpose of the study was to look at the long-term effects (defined as one year). If you had conducted this study, would you have also looked at short-term effects even if your primary objective was to look at the long-term? Explain.

4. Before reading this excerpt, would you have hypothesized that a 1½ hour group interview described above would have long-term effects on worrying by the elderly? Explain.

5. If you had planned this study, would you have included a control group? If yes, why? If no, why not?

6. If you have studied the technical language of experimental design, would you classify this study as a "true experiment," "quasi-experiment," or "pre-experiment"? Explain.

7. Are you surprised that about a third of the participants failed to return the posttests in light of the fact that they would be paid $5 to return them? Explain.

8. Does the sample size seem adequate? Explain.

9. The reduction in reported percentage of time worrying is substantial. Are you convinced that it is due to the focus group intervention? Explain.

Notes:

Case 52

Designing an Experiment on Reducing the Risk of Bulimia[1]

Problem: Researchers wanted to determine whether a group program was effective in reducing the risk of bulimia. Thus, they were interested in establishing a *cause-and-effect* relationship. They conducted the experiment described below.

Approaches to the Research Problem: One hundred seventy-seven volunteer college women were administered questionnaires to determine their risk for the development of bulimia. Twenty-nine of these women who met the criteria for being at risk for the development of bulimia and were available for participation "were randomly assigned to treatment ($n = 15$) or control ($n = 14$). Because of attrition, however, at posttest and follow-up, there were 12 participants in the treatment condition and 13 in the control condition.

"Participants assigned to treatment chose one of two group meeting times depending on their personal schedules. The effort made to equalize the number of participants in each treatment group was successful with 6 women enrolled in one group and 7 women in the other. The packet of questionnaires was re-administered 1 week (posttest) and 5 weeks (follow-up) after the end of treatment at the same time of day and on the same day of the week that the pretest (screening) was administered.

"The treatment was an 8-week structured group program designed to address the symptoms present in a sample of women at risk for bulimia. The program has been described in detail elsewhere (see McNamara, 1989); however, we did make one modification to the program. This addition consisted of a mini-lecture, suggestions, and a homework exercise that addressed participants' fears of criticism by others.

"Each session was conducted in approximately 90 minutes. Homework was assigned each week and reviewed during the following session. The first week was an introductory session, and the program's rationale was discussed in depth. The second session was primarily didactic, and the leader presented information about realistic weight goals, healthy eating habits, and the 'vicious cycle of dieting.' Cognitive interventions were introduced in the third session, and negative thinking styles were challenged. In addition, the group brainstormed about alternate, healthier ways of coping with powerful emotions and stressors. The fourth week was devoted to the relationship between perfectionism, depression, and

---

[1] Source/reference: Reprinted from Kaminski, P. L., & McNamara, K. (1996). A treatment for college women at risk for bulimia: A controlled evaluation. *Journal of Counseling & Development, 74,* 288–294. Copyright © 1996 by the American Counseling Association. Reprinted with permission.

self-esteem. In this session, participants also discussed strategies for more effectively meeting their emotional needs. During the fifth session, assertive communication strategies were discussed and difficulties in communicating directly were discussed. In the sixth session, societal pressures and messages that contribute to the prevalence of dieting behaviors and poor body esteem among women were discussed. Session seven was geared toward improving body image. Perfectionism, self-esteem, and societal pressures were reintroduced in relation to body image. In the final session, information from the preceding 7 weeks was reviewed, the group members processed their experience, and termination issues were addressed.

"The treatment groups were led by two female graduate students in counseling psychology who were supervised by a counseling psychologist. The leaders were matched in age (25 to 27 years old), ethnicity (European American), and counseling experience (2 years) and met weekly to discuss program implementation and to ensure treatment integrity. The leaders followed a written manual and attempted to adhere to the program guidelines in a similar manner to minimize the influence of unique counselor variables on outcome.

"At posttests and follow-up, participants who received the intervention reported significantly improved levels of self-esteem and body satisfaction, as well as reductions in their reliance on potentially dangerous methods of weight management compared with controls. They also reported fewer fears of negative evaluation by others and endorsed fewer stereotypes about thinness and attractiveness. Finally, participants in the treatment condition showed significantly reduced levels of perfectionism at posttest, but this change was not maintained at follow-up."

Your Opinions:

1. The study was confined to women who were at-risk for bulimia. Is this a flaw in the research methodology? Explain.

2. The participants were assigned at random to experimental and control conditions. Is this an important feature of the research methodology? Explain.

3. Is the treatment described in sufficient detail so that you could replicate the study? Explain.

4. If you have studied the technical language of experimental design, would you classify this study as a "true experiment," "quasi-experiment," or "pre-experiment"? Explain.

5. The researchers used a small sample. Is the use of a small sample ever justified when conducting an experiment? Explain.

6. Given that the leaders were supervised and followed a manual, is it important to know their gender, age, and ethnicity? Explain.

7. The follow-up was conducted at five weeks. Would an additional follow-up at a later time be desirable? If yes, how long would you suggest waiting for the additional follow-up? Explain.

8. If you have studied the technical language of experimental design, what is your opinion on the *external* and *internal validity* of the study? Is one better than the other in this experiment?

9. To what populations(s), if any, would you be willing to generalize the results of this study (i.e., to whom do these results apply)?

Notes:

Case 53

Interpreting a "Natural Experiment" on Anonymous Testing for HIV[1]

Problem: For a two-year period (called the *restriction period*), North Carolina phased out anonymous testing for HIV in 82 of 100 counties. In these 82 counties, testing became *confidential* but not anonymous. (In anonymous testing, no link exists between a person's name and the test results.) This was viewed by the state as a trial to determine whether testing rates would decline as a result of making the tests confidential instead of anonymous. The researchers' problem was to examine testing rates in the two types of counties and interpret them relative to the restriction on anonymous testing.

Findings and Interpretation: "During the study period, an HIV test was recorded 'reason for visit' for 71,434 appearances at testing sites. Of the individuals included in this category, 253 were not tested, most ($n = 238$) simply declining the test after receiving counseling (no further information was available). Before restriction, those declining a test were equally divided between the two county types; during the restriction period, however, three times as many declined in counties offering only confidential testing as in counties offering both test types (0.50% vs. 0.16%). Thus, in counties that eliminated anonymous testing, a disproportionate number of persons declined the test.

"Test seekers in the two county types were similar [with respect to gender, race, and age]. However, homosexual and bisexual men accounted for a higher percentage of tests in counties retaining vs. those eliminating anonymous testing (10% vs. 4%).

"Data on insurance status were collected...during the restriction period. Test seekers in counties retaining anonymous testing included a higher proportion with private or employer insurance than those in other counties (36% vs. 27%).

"Monthly testing increased throughout the study period... However, it increased more rapidly in counties that retained anonymous testing... In each race or gender category, testing increased more rapidly in counties where anonymous testing was retained (range of increase: 49% to 107%) than in counties where it was not (28% to 58%). A similar pattern was seen in every age group: Differences ranged from 4 to 61 percentage points. Two risk-behavior groups showed the inverse pattern of smaller increases in counties that retained anonymous testing:

[1] Source/reference: Hertz-Picciotto, I., Lee, L. W., & Hoyo, C. (1996). HIV test-seeking before and after the restriction of anonymous testing in North Carolina. *American Journal of Public Health*, *86*, 1446–1450. Copyright © 1996 American Public Health Association, Inc. Reprinted with permission.

persons with a history of sexually transmitted disease diagnosis and persons who had sex for drugs or money.

"The association between availability of anonymous testing and a greater increase in testing could be causal or either partially or wholly due to unmeasured differences between the two types of counties. Because the entire population of tests in North Carolina, rather than a random sample, was analyzed, the results do not represent 'chance' findings.

"Counties retaining anonymous testing were more urban and had more acquired immunodeficiency syndrome (AIDS) cases than the other counties, and hence residents probably were more aware of the epidemic. Also, since duplicate tests could not be identified, we could not estimate the number of repeat tests or determine whether they occurred more frequently in counties offering anonymous testing. National data indicate high rates of repeat testing over a 5-year period. Our data did not permit examination of either how frequently individuals crossed county lines to obtain an anonymous test or the extent to which persons provided false names when getting a confidential test. North Carolina does not require proof of identification for persons tested confidentially. At confidential test sites in Colorado, 27% of test seekers admitted they gave false identifying information.

"Circumstantial evidence from this study supports a detrimental effect of elimination of anonymous testing. A higher proportion of individuals declined a test after pretest counseling at sites offering only confidential testing, even though an HIV test was the recorded reason for their visit...

"Persons with private health insurance strongly preferred an anonymous test. This finding is not surprising: Confidential, positive HIV tests appear on medical records, which are accessible by court order and are routinely requested for insurance and employment applications. Studies have shown that persons with AIDS frequently lose their private health insurance and/or are refused treatment by health care providers."

Your Opinions:

1. Would it be of interest to know the basis for selecting the counties that were to phase out anonymous testing? (Note that North Carolina originally planned to eliminate anonymous testing statewide but after some controversy, decided to allow it to continue in 18 counties. Also note that the researchers state that counties retaining testing were more urban than the others.)

2. North Carolina considered this to be a "test" that would yield information to help guide policies on anonymous testing in the future. If you were setting up the study, would you have used matching to form two groups of counties that were similar, assigning one group to anonymous testing and one group to confidential testing? If yes, on what variables would you match them?

3. The researchers note that citizens of counties that retained testing may have been more aware of the epidemic. How does this affect your interpretation of the results?

4. How serious is the problem of not being able to estimate the number of repeat visits for testing?

5. How serious is the problem of not knowing how many people crossed county lines in order to be tested in counties where testing was anonymous?

6. The researchers indicate that the association "could be causal." In light of the research methodology, do you think it was probably causal? Explain.

7. The researchers indicate that their data provide only "circumstantial evidence." Do you agree? Explain.

8. In general, do you think that the data reported here are adequate for making public policy on whether testing should be anonymous? Are there other issues not studied here (in addition to the number of people tested) that might come into play when making policy? Explain.

Notes:

Notes:

Notes:

Notes:

Notes: